FUNK & WAGNALLS
NEW ILLUSTRATED ENCYCLOPEDIA OF

FAMILY HEALTH

REFERENCE EDITION

Project Editor
Sarah Bourne

Art Director
Keith Vollans

Art Editors
Kay Carroll
B Syme

Copy Editors
Penny Smith
Caroline Macy
Fiona Wilson
Jill Wiley

Index Editor
Theresa Donaghey

Managing Editor
Alan Ross

Editorial Director
Maggi McCormick

Production
Carol Milligan

Editors
Edward Horton
Felicity Smart

Deputy Editor
Elizabeth Longley

Senior Sub-editors
Anna Bradley
Sheila Brull
Arlene Sobel

Art Editor
Maggie Howells

Picture Researchers
Julia Calloway
Elizabeth Strachan
Vickie Walters

Designers
Pamela Alvares
Shirin Patel
Chris Rathbone
Jervis Tuttle
Ginger Wetherley

Artwork Researcher
Sally Walters

Production Executive
Robert Paulley

Chief Editorial Consultant
Dr. Trevor Weston,
Founder and Chairman of Health
Education Audio-Visual and Consultant
Medical Editor of the British Medical
Association's *Family Doctor*
Publications Unit. He has been both a
general practitioner and a hospital
consultant.

FUNK & WAGNALLS
NEW ILLUSTRATED ENCYCLOPEDIA OF

FAMILY HEALTH

VOLUME

13

MARSHALL CAVENDISH · LONDON · SYDNEY · NEW YORK
Distributed by Funk & Wagnalls, Inc., Ramsey, NJ

Reference Edition Published 1988
© Marshall Cavendish Limited
MCMLXXXI, MCMLXXXII, MCMLXXXIII,
MCMLXXXVI, MCMLXXXVIII

ISBN 0-86307-869-9 (Set)
ISBN 0-86307-882-6 (Vol 13)

Distributed by Funk & Wagnalls, Inc.,
Ramsey, NJ.

FUNK & WAGNALLS and F & W are
registered trademarks of Funk &
Wagnalls, Inc.

Distributed to schools and libraries by
Marshall Cavendish Corporation.

**Library of Congress Cataloging
in Publication Data**

Funk & Wagnalls new illustrated
    encyclopedia of family health.

    Rev. ed. of: The Marshall Cavendish
illustrated encyclopedia of family health.
1984.
    Includes index.
    1. Medicine, Popular—Dictionaries. I.
Funk & Wagnalls. II. Marshall
Cavendish illustrated encyclopedia of
family health. III. Title: Funk and
Wagnalls new illustrated encyclopedia
of family health.
RC81.F95 1988   610'.3'21   87-23663
ISBN 0-86307-869-9 (set)

Printed in the United States of America.

Published by Marshall Cavendish House
58 Old Compton Street
London WIV 5PA

INTRODUCTION

Our health is our most precious asset — and the health of our families is quite properly a major concern. The *Funk & Wagnalls New Illustrated Encyclopedia of Family Health* has been specially prepared to fill a unique role in this most crucial area. It is a complete and authoritative guide to your family's health, prepared by a team of experts but written in language that is clear, untechnical and straight to the point.

In every volume you will find the answers to the sort of questions you are most likely to ask, so it's really like having your own family doctor permanently on call. Not, of course, that the *Funk & Wagnalls New Illustrated Encyclopedia of Family Health* is in any sense a substitute for the enormous range of services provided by the medical profession. But doctors tell us that knowledge is the key to preventing ill health — knowledge of how our body works, knowledge of what we should and should not do to keep it in the best possible working order, and, perhaps most important of all, the knowledge that enables us to recognise any illness or disorder in its earliest stages, when medical treatment stands the greatest chance of success.

In more than 900 individual articles, arranged alphabetically for easy reference, our experts give you the inside information — dispelling myths and fallacies and replacing them with hard facts, the facts you need at your fingertips to cope with everyday health care. Each article features a special section giving the 'Doctor's' straightforward answers to the most relevant questions. Each article is fully illustrated in colour with photographs, informative diagrams and charts, to help in getting the subject across quickly, accurately, and above all, in a manner that is easily understood. A fully cross-referenced index closes Volume 23.

Volume 24 contains a quick-reference First Aid Handbook, an extensive glossary of medical terms, a complete listing of articles by volume and a classified listing of articles to help you get the most from this valuable work.

CONTENTS

Obstructions

Obstruction is a blockage in the intestine which prevents the normal flow of fluids from the stomach to the anus. Although the condition is serious there is little danger to the patient if surgery is carried out promptly.

The contents of the intestine are moved from the stomach to the anus by waves of muscular contraction. These go on 24 hours a day, but are especially vigorous just after mealtimes. Most of us swallow a lot of air with our food and the movement of the intestine is noticeable when the gas, or air, moves about too. We usually call this a tummy rumble, but doctors call it a 'bowel sound'.

Anything which obstructs the normal flow of intestinal fluids will cause trouble within hours, days or even months. The length of time taken for the symptoms to appear depends on how far down the obstruction is and how long it takes to develop.

Causes
Although the doctor can usually establish that the intestine is obstructed, he can seldom know the cause without performing special tests. However the most common cause is a trapped hernia, very often in the groin. The condition is known as a strangulated hernia and is a

This board, which hangs in the Casualty Department of Sheffield Children's Hospital, shows an amazing collection of objects that have been swallowed.

surgical emergency. Cancers also may cause obstruction either by squeezing the intestine from the outside or by invading the inside, or the obstruction may result from the intestine twisting on itself.

Symptoms
These depend on where the obstruction is. For example, with a sudden complete obstruction of the small intestine near the stomach, the first symptom is pain. The type of pain is fairly characteristic; it comes and goes and is not constant like toothache. The pain is due to the futile contractions of the muscle in the intestine as it tries to push the contents past the obstruction.

Patients often describe this as griping pain; doctors know it as colic. Fluid dams back behind the obstruction and fills the stomach. This becomes over-full and the

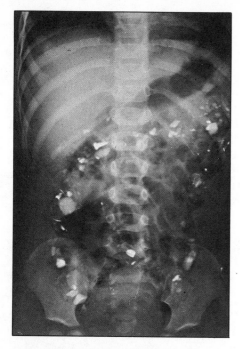

In this X-ray of a child's body we can see nails, screws and washers studded throughout the large intestine. Surgical removal is rarely necessary.

How a volvulus develops

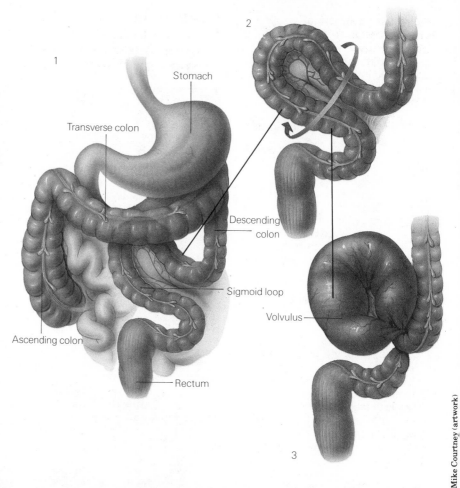

1

Stomach

Transverse colon

2

Descending colon

Sigmoid loop

Volvulus

Ascending colon

Rectum

3

patient vomits. The vomiting is distressing and profuse and little food or water is absorbed. As a result the patient rapidly becomes dehydrated and ill. Dehydration can be diagnosed from the feel of the skin, which becomes dry and inelastic.

When the obstruction is at the end of the small intestine, just before it goes into the colon (large intestine), vomiting is a late symptom. Instead, the abdomen begins to distend and there are bowel sounds. If the patient is thin enough you

(Above left) shows the whole alimentary canal and digestive tract, with an exaggerated sigmoid loop. When the loop twists, a volvulus occurs (above top), causing strangulation (above).

can actually see the strenuous efforts of the intestine through the abdominal wall as it moves the fluid past the obstruction. This is known as visible peristalsis and it is a good sign of intestinal obstruction. Because the fluid in the bowel is not kept smartly on the move it becomes infected with bacteria, usually from the colon. (The contents of the small intestine are usually fairly free of bacteria.) This infected fluid gives the breath a characteristic sweetish smell and a pungent odour to the patient's vomit.

An obstruction even further down, at the end of the colon, may be present for weeks or months before there are any

Surgical treatment is necessary to reduce intussusception: a telescoping of part of the small intestine. This kind of obstruction causes acute abdominal pain.

Q My son recently swallowed a large coin. Could this possibly cause an obstruction in his intestine?

A Yes it could, but it would be very unusual. Whatever you can swallow can normally pass through your bowel.

People can and indeed do swallow the most amazing things. It is by no means unheard of for children to swallow foreign objects such as buttons, badges, keys and marbles without causing any trouble at all. Nuts, bolts and washers are other common objects that bring patients to the Accident and Emergency Department of a hospital.

Q Can an obstruction lead to a hernia, or is it the other way round?

A It is the other way round. A hernia is a hole in the wall of the abdomen, through which the contents can be pushed. The most common place for a hernia is in the region of the groin. In most cases all that passes through the groin hernia is fat and a little of the abdominal lining. Sometimes however the hole can be large enough to admit the small intestine and when this happens it may get trapped. The condition is known as a strangulated hernia.

Q Why does abdominal pain come and go?

A Abdominal pain is caused by the rhythmical contractions of the muscle. When the intestine is obstructed, this contraction becomes more forceful; pain is felt while the muscle in contracting, and then during the period when it is relaxing the pain will tend to go away.

Q How long can a person's body tolerate obstruction before something really nasty happens?

A If the bowel is obstructed close to the stomach, symptoms develop quickly, within an hour or so, and unless something is done within 24 hours the patient lapses into quite a serious condition. However an obstruction just a short distance from the anus might not cause any symptoms for weeks.

Symptoms of obstruction

Symptom	Cause
Griping sort of pain known as colic	due to contractions of intestinal muscle as it tries to push contents of intestine past the obstruction
Vomiting	caused by concentration of fluid behind the obstruction; it eventually fills the stomach which then becomes overfull
Shock	a result of profuse vomiting; the body cannot absorb water or food and the patient becomes dehydrated
Abdominal distension	due to collection of gas and fluid in the obstructed intestine
Sweetish odour to the breath	caused by slow and partial movement of fluid through the bowel, which then becomes infected with bacteria
Tinkling bowel sounds	sound made by gas moving about in loops of intestine, which are stretched like a drum; heard only when a stethoscope is applied to the outside of the abdominal wall

major symptoms. A change in the bowel habit or progressive abdominal extension is all that may be noticed. The patient may develop diarrhoea because the liquid matter is all that can pass the obstruction.

Diagnosis
The doctor bases his diagnosis on what the patient tells him, on what he finds when he examines the abdomen and on abdominal X-rays.

One of the most important things that the surgeon has to find out is whether the patient is constipated since no faeces are passed in obstruction. The surgeon will also enquire whether the patient has passed any wind via the rectum. Normally we all pass a little bit of wind (flatus) every few hours; the absence of flatus is called absolute constipation – it is a reliable indicator of obstruction.

Abdominal distension is a sign of obstruction but it occurs in many other conditions. The sound made by the bowels, heard through a stethoscope, has a characteristic sound; it is said to make a tinkling noise and this is due to gas moving about in the loops of the intestine which is stretched like the skin of a drum.

The surgeon relies heavily on the X-ray of the abdomen to confirm the diagnosis. Two pictures are taken: one with the patient lying flat and one with the patient sitting up. When the bowel is obstructed, pools of stagnant intestinal fluid are formed; there is also a moderate amount of gas in the small intestine. When the

patient sits up the fluid will form little pools in the loops of the intestine with pockets of gas above them. These interfaces between the fluid and the gas show up as a 'fluid level' on the X-ray and confirm the presence of obstruction.

Dangers
The condition is not dangerous provided that surgery is performed promptly. In the past, when anaesthetics were not good enough to allow abdominal surgery, everyone suffering from this condition died due to loss of fluid and shock.

Anaesthetics are now very safe and although surgery has an element of danger, it is only really risky in those who are very old or very frail. Nevertheless, obstruction can be very difficult for the surgeon to deal with if it has been present for a long time.

Treatment and outlook
Obstructions are only rarely caused by swallowing coins or paper clips; these will be evacuated naturally and require no treatment. When an obstruction does occur from another cause, an operation will be needed. If the patient is dehydrated and vomiting the surgeon will make every effort to improve the condition before the operation. During surgery the obstructed piece of bowel may have to be removed and the cut ends on either side are joined end to end. The outlook for treatment depends upon the seriousness of what caused the condition in the first place; however usually it is good.

Occupational hazards

Q I read somewhere that inhaling certain dusts, rather than all dusts, is dangerous. Why?

A While it is certainly not desirable to have any foreign particles entering the lungs, some dusts are more dangerous than others. A stonemason who works only with marble and inhales its dust has practically no chance of getting lung disease, but if he were chipping away at sandstone, the risk of lung disease and death caused by the dust would be very great. The reason for these differences is not fully understood. However there are many dusts, such as asbestos, that are a special danger and can cause cancer of the lung and the pleura (lining of the lung), as well as the disabling disease asbestosis. However the use of asbestos in industry is now strictly controlled.

Q Are Visual Display Terminals at all harmful? My wife uses one and we have heard mixed reports about their safety?

A The reports on VDT health risks are very mixed but there is increasing evidence that prolonged use of VDTs may cause operators to have health problems. These range from eyestrain, headaches, pains in the back, neck, arms and fingers, to general stress symptoms. Many of these problems are all alleviated if the VDT is set in a properly designed work-station, and regular breaks are taken, away from the screen. At least 15 minutes' rest every hour is recommended. Statistics also show that a high proportion of pregnant VDT operators suffer from miscarriages or malformed babies. This should be considered if you wish to start a family.

Q We have a union safety representative in our office. Why do we need one?

A Every year thousands of office staff are injured at work. Half the injuries are caused by falls, by tripping over either trailing wires or carelessly placed objects on stairs. Accidents such as these are largely preventable. A safety representative can assess potential dangers to office staff.

Every year, occupational hazards cause illness, injury and sometimes death among a nation's workforce. What are these hazards and can they be prevented?

Health hazards associated with work have been known for centuries, but it was only in the last two hundred years, with the development of industrialization, that a multitude of occupational hazards were either created or came to light. And although industry was slow to recognize and deal with them, safety measures are now regarded as a priority by employers and trade unions alike.

Quite apart from the personal toll that occupational disease and injury can bring, there is a heavy economic price to pay. In Great Britain, in 1978, over 15 million working days were lost through work-related injuries and illness.

Many of the most serious occupational hazards have been brought under control by legislation such as the Factories Act and the Health and Safety at Work Act in Great Britain. But risk can never be entirely eliminated if new products are to be developed and society is to progress.

Further, accidents with machinery can never be totally avoided because of human error. However they can be minimized if employers ensure that the standards of safety are maintained, and if workers adhere to safety regulations.

Zefa

Types of hazards
Hazards may be in the form of gas, liquids or solids. They can enter the body through the lungs, by contact with the skin and by ingestion through the mouth.
Dangerous metals: Lead, a most notorious toxic substance, is used in the manufacture of batteries, rubber, paint, roofing and soldering material. It can enter the body through inhalation of small dust particles and fumes, or by ingestion (see pp 963-5).

The first symptoms may include tiredness, headache, loss of appetite, constipation and mild abdominal pain.

Clearly some jobs are far more dangerous than others. Mining (left) and construction work (above) are inherently hazardous in terms of risks to life and limb.

Extreme poisoning—rare nowadays—can result in severe abdominal pain, muscle weakness, kidney damage, convulsions, coma and death.

Mercury, a silver-coloured liquid used in thermometers, is another hazardous metal. It is utilized in the electrical industry in the manufacture of fluorescent lamps and of precision instruments, and in dentistry.

Mercury poisoning causes jerky movements starting in the fingers, irritability, drowsiness and, in the final stage, madness. Other symptoms are sore throat and gums, vomiting and diarrhoea. Compounds from mercury can also be dangerous when they occur in the form of industrial effluents which are absorbed, for instance, by the fish we eat. These can cause blindness, mental deterioration, lack of co-ordination, birth defects and death.

Cadmium, a soft metal used for increasing the hardness of copper and as a protective plating for other metals, is particularly dangerous because once someone has inhaled or ingested a certain amount there is no known cure. Poisoning can be gradual because the amount of metal in the body slowly builds up. At a critical point the lungs and the

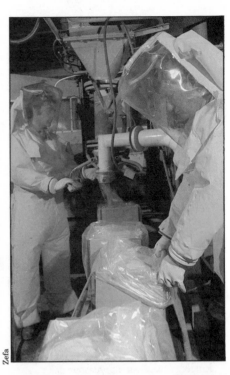

Deep sea diving (above left) has more obvious risks than other jobs in industries, such as smelting (below) and chemical manufacturing (above right) where the risks are less apparent but can still cause disease, disablement and death. For this reason laws relating to safety have been created to prevent serious injuries.

Q I am a shiftworker. Will it affect my health?

A Shiftworking affects people in different ways. About 20 per cent of people actually enjoy working nights, whereas another 20 per cent dislike it intensely and have to give it up. No studies have shown any difference in causes of death between day and shiftworkers, and indeed most studies have revealed that shiftworkers have fewer sickness absences. However if you were previously working during the day, it will take time for your body to adapt to working nights. Problems can include digestive disorders, fatigue and an increase in accidents.

Q I work near a very hot furnace. Am I in danger?

A Normally the body can adapt to raised temperatures, but if your job also involves heavy physical labour and if the salt and water lost during sweating is not replaced, you may suffer from heat-stroke, or heat syncope, both of which cause collapse. Heat-stroke can be expected at 29°C (84.2°F). Treatment involves cooling the body and rest. However if you become acclimatized to the high temperature, your heat tolerance is likely to be greater and the chance of heat-stroke reduced.

Q I am a heavy smoker who works as a plasterer. Will smoking increase the risk of getting a work-related disease?

A Yes. For instance, an asbestos worker is three times as likely to get lung cancer as a non-asbestos worker, but if he also smokes, his chances of dying from the disease are 90 times greater than someone who does not smoke and does not work with asbestos. Smoking itself damages the airways, the natural defence of the lungs; this will allow easier access of harmful substances.

Q Why are substances known to cause cancer used in industry?

A Unfortunately, this is a fact of life if we want new products and progress. However, exposure to carcinogenic material is strictly limited to what experts believe is as safe a level as possible.

kidneys cease to function properly and death can result.

Chromium, a silver-white, hard, brittle metal, is used to make various steels, including stainless steel, and high speed tools. Its compounds are used in chrome plating, in the production of pigments in paints and inks, in leather tanning agents, in timber preservation and in photography and dyestuffs.

The danger of chromium is that even slight contact with dilute solutions can cause skin ulcers.

The inhalation of fine droplets or mist containing chromium salts can cause ulcers inside the nose. Although lung cancer has not been associated with chrome plating, it has been linked with the manufacture of chromates. Asthmatic symptoms can also occur, as can chrome sensitivity: a strong reaction to chrome following symptoms of exposure.

Solvents: There are many liquids classed as solvents and workers in nearly all occupations are exposed to them, from the office typist to the engineer. Solvents evaporate very quickly, and the vapours can enter the body by being inhaled through the lungs, through the skin and more rarely, through the digestive system. Once they enter the body, they can attack the liver, the heart, the lungs and the nervous system.

Solvents are found in inks, varnishes, glues, cleaners, dry cleaning fluids and many other substances. Some of the most dangerous ones may be very pleasant to smell, whereas others that are foul-smelling may be quite harmless.

Trichloroethylene smells very nice but it can lead to loss of consciousness and death. Benzene is another pleasant smelling solvent used in the manufacture of artificial leather, lino detergents, pesticides and paint removers. It can cause dizziness and coma or, when poisoning is chronic, leukaemia.

Because of the dissolving properties of solvents, they can attack the skin and cause dermatitis (see Dermatitis, pp 369-70). Contact with solvents should be strictly limited.

Unlike solvents, all isocynanates are dangerous. They are used in the manufacture of polyurethanes which make foams, adhesives, lacquers and paints.

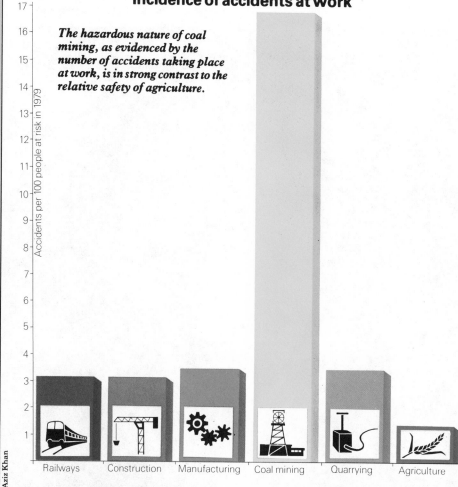

Incidence of accidents at work

The hazardous nature of coal mining, as evidenced by the number of accidents taking place at work, is in strong contrast to the relative safety of agriculture.

Accidents per 100 people at risk in 1979

Railways Construction Manufacturing Coal mining Quarrying Agriculture

Aziz Khan

Over-exposure to isocynanates in the air can lead to skin inflammations, eye irritations and breathing difficulties, including severe asthma. People can also develop isocynanate-sensitivity.

Dusts: Dust is the biggest killer in industry. However, some dusts are relatively harmless, while others are deadly.

There are four basic categories of dust. The first is nuisance or inert dust such as plaster of Paris, starch and Portland cement. These can accumulate in the body without producing a serious reaction. Toxic dusts include lead and chromium compounds. They can have serious effects on specific organs in the body like the kidneys and the nervous system. Dusts that produce allergic-type reactions, such as some wood dusts and fungus spores from grain, can cause asthma and eczema. Finally dusts that change the lung tissue, like asbestos and coal dust, make the lungs inefficient, and each year cause death and serious disability in hundreds of people.

The danger of dusts depends not only on the type of dust but on the amount and the time over which it is breathed. Breathing a lot of dust in a short time can be more harmful than breathing a little over a long time.

Healthy lungs can cope with a certain amount of dust and fumes with no ill effects. However the body's defence mechanisms cannot cope with the onslaught of dangerous or excessive dusts. This is why elimination of dust in the working atmosphere is so important, and why protective clothing and respiratory equipment must be used.

Noise: In many industries working with a deafening din was accepted as part of the job. Nowadays noise, though inescap-

Laboratory accidents leading to contamination can be avoided by following safety procedures.

Zefa

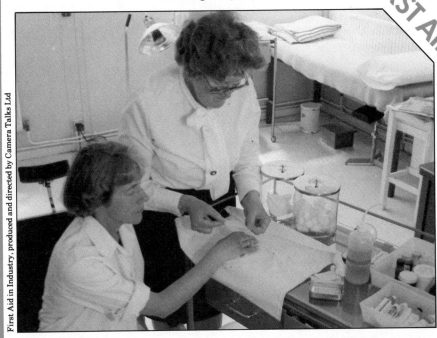

First Aid in Industry, produced and directed by Camera Talks Ltd

Emergency first aid

If you have to give first aid in an emergency, first check whether the patient is breathing. If breathing has stopped, start mouth-to-mouth resuscitation at once before giving any other treatment. Second, check for serious bleeding. Control bleeding by pressing at the site of the wound with a sterilized pad or with your fingers. Raise the injured limb, if possible, to help slow the blood flow. Third, if the patient is unconscious, make sure he or she can breathe and that the throat is not obstructed. Then place the person in the recovery position. Seek expert help immediately.

Other injuries	Treatment
Burns and scalds	Cool the area by flushing with plenty of clean, cool water. Then cover with a sterile dressing or clean material. Do not apply any ointment, burst any blisters or remove any clothing sticking to burns
Chemical burns	Remove contaminated clothing—taking care not to contaminate yourself—and dilute chemical by flushing with plenty of water. Then apply dry dressing
Chemical in the eye	Quickly flush the open eye with clean, cool water. Continue for at least ten minutes
Foreign body in the eye	If the object cannot easily be removed with the corner of a clean piece of material or by flushing with water, send the patient to hospital
Broken bones	Unless there is danger of further injury, do not move the patient until expert help arrives
Electric shock	Do not touch patient until the current has been switched off. If breathing has stopped, give mouth-to-mouth resuscitation and call for expert help
Gassing	Move patient into fresh air, but wear suitable breathing equipment so that you do not become a patient yourself. If breathing has stopped, give mouth-to-mouth resuscitation
Amputation of finger	Keep pressure over stump to prevent arterial bleeding. Wrap up finger—with ice if possible. Rush patient to hospital

Q I have heard that if a husband works with dangerous substances his wife can sometimes be affected. Is this really true?

A Yes. This can occur if proper precautions and personal hygiene are not attended to. Cases of lead poisoning, for instance, have been seen among families of lead workers who went home without changing their overalls. Asbestos workers can also carry home fibres on their clothes, and put their families at risk. However strict regulations normally ensure that such risks are a thing of the past.

Q I work in industry but am planning to start a family. Are there any health risks that could affect my pregnancy?

A There are laws to protect women against the most dangerous hazards to pregnancy, such as lead. Other risks include waste anaesthetic gases which operating theatre staff are exposed to and which can cause abortions and birth defects; radiation, to which a foetus is 10 times as vulnerable as an adult; and mercury and its compounds, which can produce mental abnormalities in offspring. It should be remembered that the foetus is at risk from all toxic substances that are transferred via the mother, and this is why even smoking and drinking alcohol during pregnancy can be dangerous.

Q I use a pneumatic drill whose noise level is well controlled. Could the vibrations affect my body in any way?

A The major hazard for people using vibration tools is vibration white finger. The blood supply to the fingers is impeded and the fingers appear pale and may tingle and feel numb. At a certain stage, the fingers do not return to normal. Workers with poor circulation of the blood should not do this sort of job. Others should wear warm clothing and padded gloves when using the tools and, where possible, work in a warm environment to ensure good circulation of the extremities. Hours for this type of work should be limited.

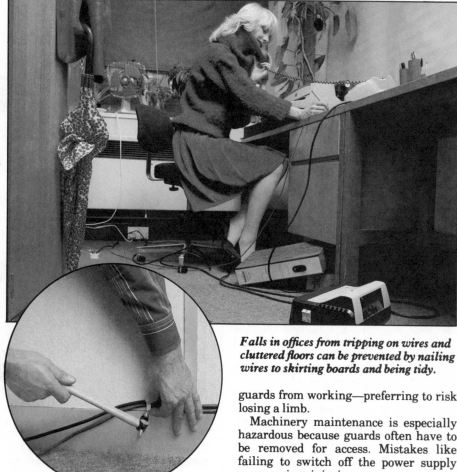

Falls in offices from tripping on wires and cluttered floors can be prevented by nailing wires to skirting boards and being tidy.

able in many industries, is viewed as a occupational hazard for which there are controls and preventive measures.

The basic preventive measure is to cut the noise of machinery at source by deadening its sound, and by instructing workers to wear appropriate ear muffs or plugs. Though many workers resist wearing them, they drastically reduce the sound reaching the ear.

Occupational injuries

In Britain every year, thirty out of every million people employed in ordinary factory jobs die as a result of an occupational accident or disease. Certainly some jobs have a high death-risk factor, for instance steeplejacking or working on North Sea oil rigs, but others, while not in themselves as dangerous, involve machinery that if misused can give rise to accidents. In 1979, over 22,000 accidents with machinery in factories were reported; 37 of these were fatal.

A proportion of these accidents occurred through the use of unguarded machinery. Although all machinery must by law be guarded, some employers, in an attempt to cut corners, do not ensure that this is done. Moreover some workers, like those on piecework, who believe that the guard is slowing their output and losing them pay, deliberately prevent

guards from working—preferring to risk losing a limb.

Machinery maintenance is especially hazardous because guards often have to be removed for access. Mistakes like failing to switch off the power supply cause serious injuries.

Over 12,000 injuries in British factories in 1979 were caused through the use of hand tools. Particularly common were eye injuries from fragments of metal flying off drills or chips of stone or metal split off while hammering. Wearing eye protection—however much disliked— would have prevented this type of injury.

Certain types of hand tools such as chainsaws can be responsible for a disease known as vibration white finger. The symptoms are pallor spreading down from the fingertips and a tingling sensation. This can progress to a blue tingeing of the fingers and sometimes pain or loss of sensation. There is unfortunately no known cure for white finger. Workers using vibration tools should wear padded gloves and keep their hands warm.

Finally, falls in factories account for a high proportion of occupational injuries. Most of these falls occurred on a level floor, and were mainly due to gangways being cluttered with boxes, spilt liquids not mopped up and sheer untidiness.

Falls also account for half of the 5000 serious injuries suffered by office staff in Great Britain every year. Trailing wires, filing cabinet drawers left open, and poorly lit stairs are all traps.

Many injuries can be prevented by following safety regulations, wearing safety equipment, better office and factory housekeeping and simple care.

Occupational hazards

Hazard	Industry	Mode of entry	Symptoms	Treatment	Prevention
Asbestos	Numerous, including ship-building, pipe and boiler lagging, building	Inhalation	Breathlessness, dry cough, cancer of the lung or pleura (lining of thorax and lungs)	Remove from further exposure and relieve symptoms	Enclosure of dust producing process; personal protection; monitoring the work environment; using substitute materials
Cadmium	Plating on metals, production of alloys, paints, enamel and pigments	Inhalation or ingestion	Irritation of eyes and nose, breathlessness, vomiting, diarrhoea, colic, coughing, headache, kidney damage	Symptomatic only	Enclosure of the process; personal protection; environmental monitoring
Chromium	Car industry, steel, pigments, leather tanning, photography	Inhalation	Ulcers on skin especially nasal membrane, asthmatic symptoms in some	Ointment and local treatment of ulcers	Enclosure of the process; personal protection; environmental monitoring
Hepatitis	Laboratory and hospital workers	Contact with infected blood or excreta	Weakness, loss of appetite, malaise, jaundice	No specific treatment; usually self-limiting disease	Personal disinfectant and protection
Isocynanates	Polyurethane manufacture, adhesives, synthetic rubbers, paints, lacquers, urethane foams	Vapour inhalation or contact with skin	Dermatitis, coughing, eye irritation, breathlessness and asthma	Removal from contact, symptomatic treatment	Exhaust ventilation; personal protection
Lead	Batteries, rubber, paint, roofing and soldering	Ingestion, inhalation	Tiredness, headache, loss of appetite, paleness, constipation, pain in the abdomen, muscle weakness, kidney damage, convulsions, coma	Removal from exposure, chelating elements that remove lead and change its properties, oral pericillamine	Exhaust ventilation; personal hygiene; environmental monitoring; regular analysis of blood and urine samples
Mercury	Electrical industry, fluorescent lamps, precision instruments, dentistry	Inhalation, ingestion, absorption through skin	Jerky movements, irritability, drowsiness, bleeding gums, madness	Removal from source of contact	Enclosure of process; exhaust ventilation; personal protection
Noise	Drop-forging, boiler-making, ship-building		Deafness	Remove from further exposure	Reduce noise of machinery; personal protection
Radiation	Medicine, welding checks, atomic energy and weapons, luminous dials	Irradiation through the body, ingestion of the contaminated particles	Burns, scaling of skin, loss of hair, cancer, cataracts, dermatitis, genetic damage	Symptomatic; immediate removal from contamination	Screening from source; monitoring; personal protection
Silicosis	Pottery, mining, quarrying, sand-blasting	Inhalation	Dry cough, breathlessness, bronchitis, extreme respiratory disablement	Remove from further exposure, treat symptoms	Personal protection; damping dust; enclosing process
Solvents	Inks, varnishes, glues, degreasing agents dry cleaning, paints	Inhalation, skin contact, ingestion	Numerous: damage to nervous system, liver, heart, lungs, dermatitis	Various. Remove from exposure	Exhaust ventilation; monitoring environment; using personal protection
Vibration	Building, welding, forestry	Contact with tool	Pale, numb fingers	Removal from contact	Personal protection; work in warm enviroment; padded gloves
Wood dust	Furniture, wood polishers, wood yards	Inhalation and contact with skin	Dermatitis, respiratory irritation, rare variety of nasal cancer	Symptomatic	Dust extraction; personal protection

Occupational therapy

Q Since my wife had a stroke her right arm is almost useless. She would like to be more independent but finds that trying to cook and do housework with only one good hand is slow and frustrating. Can anyone help her?

A The occupational therapy department in your local hospital will have a kitchen unit with a variety of gadgets to make one-handed cooking and housework easier. The occupational therapist will also check whether your wife needs help with other tasks like dressing and washing and provide assistance.

Q My husband has had a nervous breakdown. Will he need occupational therapy?

A Often a breakdown happens because of the difficulty of coping with the stresses of everyday life. Occupational therapy will help people become more competent. This may involve encouraging self-confidence in social skills, for instance in talking to or in front of other people. It may mean helping someone who has not worked for some time get used to working alongside other people and begin to accept responsibilities again.

Q I am frightened of having a bath because I find it difficult to get out of the tub. Can anything be done to help me?

A An occupational therapist from the local social services department can be asked to come and see you. She will analyze the problem and may suggest aids to help you, like a non-slip mat and a bath seat and perhaps a rail on the wall above the bath. She can arrange for these to be supplied and would then teach you how to use them.

Q Why did my child need occupational therapy in hospital when recovering from pneumonia?

A Any long stay in hospital is boring, and so potentially demoralizing. A depressed patient never recovers so quickly, or finds it so easy to adjust to the outside world.

Occupational therapy is the use of selected activities to help people of all ages with a disability or handicap reach their maximum level of function and independence – in all aspects of daily life.

Some occupational therapists work mainly with physically disabled patients. They are concerned with mobilizing stiff joints, strengthening muscles, improving co-ordination and building up stamina. Therapists may use activities such as planing wood to exercise a weak back, treadling a foot-powered lathe to exercise the legs or working a hand printing press to strengthen an arm.

Therapists also help patients who have difficulty with day-to-day activities such as getting in and out of the bath and cutting up food. In most occupational therapy departments there will be a kitchen, bathroom and bedroom section where patients can try out aids and practise new techniques.

Occupational therapists also treat mentally ill and mentally handicapped people. Therapists use activities like painting and music which provide opportunities for self-expression. They use discussion groups and social activities to help shy and withdrawn patients express themselves better and relate to others. They use shopping and cooking and work activities to help patients cope with living in the community.

Occupational therapists work with social services departments to help the handicapped live at home. This may mean arranging for the provision of aids such as extended legs to make an armchair higher, or adaptations like a second banister rail. Or their duties may include working with architects to plan major alterations like a downstairs bathroom suitable for someone who is in a wheelchair.

Equally, occupational therapists may work in day centres where patients with a physical disability, mental illness or mental handicap can go to meet other patients and enjoy a change in environment.

Benefits

Patients with a temporary disability, like a hand injury, will need occupational therapy to get their hand moving again as quickly as possible so they can return to work.

People with a long-term illness, like arthritis, will need occupational therapy to help them cope with all the practical and psychological problems they are going to have to face.

Penny Tweedie

Patients who have had to go into a mental hospital because of depression, anxiety, irrational thoughts and fears or for many other reasons will need occupational therapy as an integral part of their treatment.

Patients who are handicapped and living at home and who are isolated or unable to look after themselves will need an occupational therapist to help them improve their quality of life.

Elderly people who tend to sit in a chair at home doing nothing, and begin to lose the ability to do things they could manage before, can also benefit from occupational therapy. It can stimulate them into wanting to do more for themselves and also show them easier ways of accomplishing many minor but essential tasks round the house.

Therapy at home and in hospital

In a general hospital, occupational therapists work as part of the treatment team alongside doctors, nurses and physiotherapists. They may initially see patients on the wards but usually treatment will be continued in the hospital occupational therapy department. The occupational therapists will often make home visits before their patients are discharged to find out whether they will be able to manage. If there are problems the occupational therapist will contact the appropriate person in the social services. Some people will attend occupational therapy as out-patients provided they can get to the hospital.

Some forms of treatment are available in special units. Among these are rehabilitation centres where intensive daily treatment is available, and children's units, day hospitals for the elderly, stroke units, spinal injuries units and burns units. Occupational therapists are usually part of the treatment team in all these. They are also beginning to work in special schools specifically for handicapped children.

In psychiatric hospitals occupational therapists work with psychiatrists and psychologists. In the large old-fashioned hospitals there are usually a number of occupational therapy departments serving different types of patients. In the smaller modern units attached to general hospitals, the occupational therapists may be working in their own department or on the wards or in special units treating drug addicts or alcoholics. Alternatively they may work in a therapeutic community or use specific techniques like behaviour modification for patients with psychological problems. In hospitals for the mentally handicapped, occupational therapists will help patients develop social skills.

In the community, occupational therapists are usually attached to an area social work team where they work alongside social workers but take special responsibility for the handicapped. Some occupational therapists either work in or run day centres for handicapped people.

Here are shown just some of the applications of occupational therapy: older people (far left) are finding both companionship and mental stimulation in a handicraft session; these young boys (left), faced with a long hospital stay, are being helped to be as physically and mentally active as they can—and so speed recovery. In a psychiatric hospital, the occupational therapist has a vital role, typically directing 'industrial therapy' as a form of rehabilitation (below, left). Painting provides an outlet for self-expression, and is useful as a part of total treatment.

Anthea Sievking/Vision International

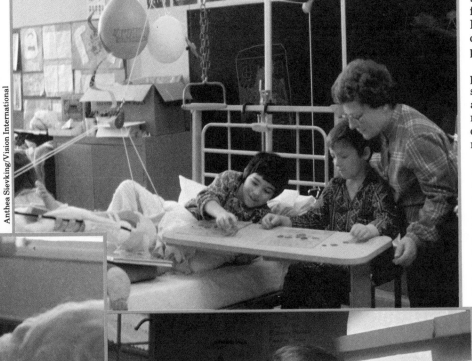

C.O.I. Photos

Colorific!

RONSEAL

Oedema

Areas of swelling indicate a fault in the body's drainage system. It is usually due to heart or liver disease, but can have other causes.

Roger Payling

All blood vessels leak just a little fluid which collects outside them. Normally this fluid is removed by an efficient drainage system, the lymphatic vessels (see pp 1072-75), but when the system fails the fluid builds up and the conditon is known as oedema (edema).

Causes

Fluid leaks out of blood vessels because the walls of the vessels are thin and the blood that circulates around the body is being pumped by the heart under considerable pressure. Fluid returns to the blood vessels by a process known as osmosis.

Osmosis takes place when fluid passes

Mild oedema leading to swollen ankles can be helped by elastic stockings which squeeze fluid out of the affected area. But any swelling of the joints, including ankles, should be reported to your doctor.

from a weak solution to a strong solution across a semi-permeable membrane. The walls of blood vessels form semi-permeable membranes, and within these vessels flows a strong solution of proteins, the natural constituents of blood. It is these proteins that are responsible for sucking back in a lot of the fluid that has seeped out.

Lack of protein in the blood resulting from malnutrition or liver disease is a common cause of oedema. Obstruction of the drainage system—either the lymphatic vessels or the veins—also leads to the accumulation of fluid because of a build-up in pressure. As a consequence, thrombosis and varicose veins are sometimes causes of ankle swelling. Heart failure can lead to a backlog of blood in the veins. When the kidneys fail to remove excessive salt from the blood, or if we eat too much salt with fluids, the volume of fluid in the blood vessels increases greatly, and so does the rate at which fluid leaks out.

The rate at which salt is passed into the urine—assuming the kidneys are functioning properly—is regulated by the adrenal hormones. The balance of these is altered during pregnancy and menstruation: at these times slight oedema may result from salt retention.

Special types of oedema

Gravity determines where oedema occurs. The most common place is around the ankles, but after a patient has spent a long period in bed oedema fluid may collect around the buttocks or sacrum.

Severe heart failure, liver failure or obstruction of any of the large veins in the abdomen cause fluid to collect inside the abdominal cavity. This is known as ascites.

Similarly, fluid accumulates in the lungs if the left side of the heart fails. This causes severe breathlessness with a cough and frothy sputum and requires emergency attention.

Symptoms

Ankle oedema is easy to see if the ankles are grossly swollen, but slight swelling can be more difficult to detect. Fluid tends to collect first on the inner side of the ankle, just behind the ankle bone. Breathlessness at rest is a symptom of pulmonary oedema, when the lungs become filled with fluid.

Dangers

Ankle oedema is not dangerous in itself but it may be a symptom of a more serious condition such as heart disease which requires treatment. Pulmonary oedema, however, if severe is a medical emergency, for if not treated quickly the patient will become extremely short of breath, as it were drowning in his own oedema fluid. Prompt drug treatment will lead to almost certain recovery.

Treatment

Oedema caused by leakage from ageing and thin blood vessels can be controlled by wearing an elastic stocking which squeezes the fluid out of the ankles. If the fundamental cause is heart failure,

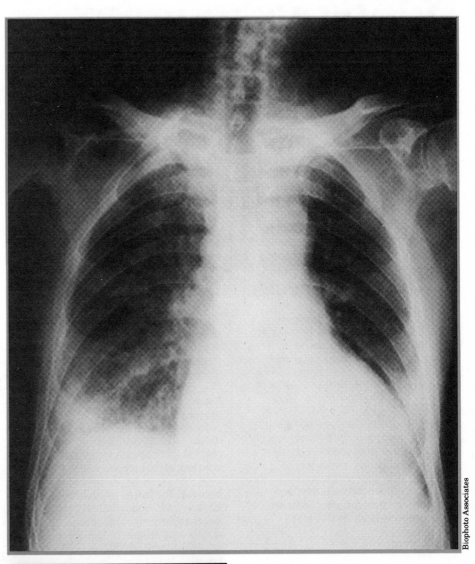

Biophoto Associates

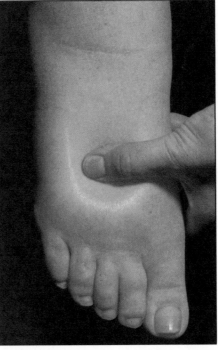

The X-ray (above) shows lungs containing fluid as a result of pulmonary oedema. This condition is treated by a diuretic injected into the vein.

Oedema of the foot and ankle (left) gives rise to a swelling pronounced enough for a dent to be left after finger pressure.

however, the main approach is to reduce the volume of blood circulating around the body in order to reduce the strain on the heart. This is done by taking tablets, known as diuretics, which make the patient pass water and reduce the level of salt. The process is aided if the patient refrains from adding salt when cooking, and it is sometimes necessary to take a potassium supplement.

Pulmonary oedema is treated with a fast-acting diuretic which is given intravenously. Oxygen given through a mask may also be necessary. Thrombosis of the veins is treated by thinning of the blood with anti-coagulants. Varicose veins can be removed surgically.

Oedipus complex

Q In our family the Oedipus complex seems to be reversed. My 14-year-old son is very close to his father but extremely aggressive towards me as his mother. Is this unusual?

A At your son's age a mother-son antagonism is common. By establishing his independence of you he proclaims his masculinity, a set of attitudes that is probably reflected in his friends' behaviour which he may well be apeing.

Q Is it normal for the Oedipus complex to persist into adulthood?

A An adult wish to have sex with one's opposite-sex parent and a fear of retribution by sexual maiming at the hands of the parent of the same sex is not at all normal. Some psychologists, however, believe that many of us have such thoughts buried deep and that the resulting anxiety produces many fears in adult life. Others deny this, saying most people never have the Oedipus complex in the first place.

Q I've heard it said that the Oedipus complex leads to homosexuality. Is this true?

A There is evidence that an over-possessive mother and a distant or hostile father can lead to a child becoming homosexual. Whether a classic Oedipus complex is involved is debatable, but if the child lacks a strong and helpful male father-figure on which to model his own masculinity, his ability to behave in a sexually conventional manner will be limited and may, in time, lead to homosexuality.

Q Can women have an Oedipus complex?

A Freud's female equivalent of Oedipus is found in the Electra complex, where the young girl is sexually attracted to her father, regarding the mother as a hostile rival. The repression of these feelings is said to produce a preoccupation with sex, yet a fear and avoidance of it, in practice.

Sigmund Freud made an immense impact on 20th-century thought, not least by putting forward the controversial theory that sons may develop an excessive attachment to their mothers – the Oedipus complex.

Sigmund Freud (1856—1939) is considered the father of modern psychology, since he laid down the basis for psycho-analytical theory while investigating the inner workings of the human mind. Freud developed a whole series of ideas, based on the observation of his own patients, as to why we behave as we do. Although he never tried to prove scientifically any of his theories, many of his ideas live on today, still controversial and still debated. The Oedipus complex is one of Freud's best-known concepts.

To find the vehicle that best described his theory, Freud borrowed from Greek legend. The term Oedipus complex derives from the story of Oedipus, a Theban hero who grew up not knowing the identity of his true parents. Unknowingly, he later slew his father, and married his mother.

In describing the parallel female condition, Freud returned to the world of mythology, borrowing the name Electra, who helped to slay her mother.

Sexual feelings in childhood

Freud believed that during sexual development a child passes through a number of stages in which the focus of sexual attention is successively the mouth, the anus, then the penis or clitoris. At this last stage, supposed to happen at about the age of four, the child becomes sexually attracted to the parent of the opposite sex. Believing opposition might come from the same-sex parent, the child imagines that this parent will punish these desires by sexual mutilation—in the case of a boy, by the act of castration.

Fearing this punishment, the boy rejects his mother as a potential sexual partner and identifies himself with his

It sometimes happens that a man fails to outlive his childhood dependence on his mother. He grows up an over-dutiful son, enjoying the care and attention of a doting mother who is flattered by her son's continuing display of affection and concern. Sigmund Freud suggested that the Oedipus complex involved a boy having feelings of sexual desire towards his mother, but many modern-day psychologists believe that Freud was wrong in this theory and that dependence on a mother doesn't necessarily reflect sexual desire.

father, saying in effect: 'Believe me, I don't desire the object of your love. I'm on your side.' The desire is repressed, but the feeling and the 'lie' about it hang over the child and create sexual guilt and anxiety.

Such is Freud's theory, but finding evidence to prove it is not easy. Freud said that most males overcome the conflict, moving on to more appropriate sexual objects and realizing that their sexuality is not threatened by the father. Many modern psychologists and psychiatrists disagree totally with the theories of Freud on this and say children never harbour Oedipal desires and fears towards or about their mothers.

Tied to mother's apron strings

Even the strongest critics of Freud agree he was right in one sense anyway. Most doctors know of men, especially, who are devoted to their mothers and who are cool or hostile towards their fathers. Such a man may not have feelings of sexual desire towards his mother but in many other ways he behaves like a too-dutiful husband—constantly bringing gifts, worried about introducing other women to her, feeling guilty if he 'deserts' her for any length of time, and so on. Over-dependence on a mother and comparative disdain of father is directly comparable to what Freud would have called an Oedipal problem.

The case of a daughter identifying too closely with her father—called by Freud the Electra complex—occurs less frequently. When it does happen the girl is often over-dependent on males in general.

Some psychiatrists also believe that the popularity of the 'bitch-goddess' figure in male erotic fantasy denotes the symbolic representation of an Oedipus complex that has not been fully resolved. In this case, the man's desire is totally sexual and focuses upon some of his mother's qualities—dominance, punishment, restriction and coolness—that she displayed to him as a child.

Treatment

The maternally-dependent male often goes undetected until he comes under stress from another source. If this stress comes from his wife—who will often be partly a mother-figure as well—then the difficulties become particularly acute. As one psychiatrist has put it, the problem is big enough to bring about a divorce yet seldom sufficiently acute to bring the person in for treatment.

If the man believes that sexual desire for his mother is involved (together with hostility and fear of his father) it may be necessary for him to have his anxiety treated by a therapist. If, instead, he is excessively dependent on his mother, a programme aimed at building up the patient's self-esteem and independence may help to lessen the degree of dependence and reduce the restrictions on his life. Such an aim, however is sometimes not easy to achieve, for the mother may feel the loss of her son's over-solicitous support very keenly and may strongly resist his attempts to untie himself from her apron strings by emotional blackmail of various kinds.

It cannot be expected that the mother would become involved in the therapy situation, so if the break from her is achieved, it is sometimes very difficult and dramatic.

Roger Payling

Oesophagus

Q If I drink something that is too hot, can I actually burn my oesophagus?

A In theory, yes, you can; in practice this happens very rarely indeed. The nerve endings in your lips, tongue and the lining of your mouth would have warned you that the liquid was painfully hot and you would have stopped drinking and spat out any already in your mouth before it was swallowed.

Q If my baby son accidentally swallows something sharp, like a piece of broken glass, what damage could be done to the oesophagus?

A Usually, amazingly little damage is done, even though one would have thought that some dramatic disaster was virtually certain. Sometimes the glass scratches the lining of the oesophagus as it goes down and causes a little bleeding, but seldom more than that. If something like this does happen, however, it would be wise to let your doctor know. It may be necessary to follow the foreign body's progress through the gut, and possibly take X-rays to see where it has got to until it has been excreted.

Q Can anything be done for people suffering from cancer of the oesophagus?

A Yes, a great deal. There are now a large number of people alive many years after being successfully treated for cancer of the oesophagus. Provided that the diagnosis is made early—and this is the crucial factor—a curative operation is usually possible.

If the cancer is in the lower part of the oesophagus, the operation will consist of removing the cancerous section and bringing up the stomach to be joined with the cut end. Growths in the upper part of the oesophagus used to be much more difficult to deal with because there is not so much room for manoeuvre. But nowadays it is sometimes possible to overcome this difficulty by transplanting part of the colon to act as a replacement for the diseased section of the oesophagus.

Most food passes down the oesophagus so smoothly that we are unaware of its passage. It is only when we eat something too large, too hot or too cold that we notice this vital link between mouth and stomach.

The oesophagus or gullet is the tube that connects the back of the mouth to the stomach. Its only function is to carry food from the mouth to the parts of the alimentary canal in the abdomen where it will be broken down by the various digestive processes and then absorbed into the bloodstream.

Structure

The top of the oesophagus lies immediately behind the trachea or windpipe. Just below the level of the notch at the top of the chest, the tube bends slightly to the left and passes behind the left bronchus. It then goes through the diaphragm and connects with the upper end of the stomach.

The entrance to the stomach is controlled by a muscular ring that closes to prevent food being forced back up the oesophagus by the forceful contractions of the stomach.

The oesophagus is an elastic tube about 25 cm (10 in) long and about 2.5 cm (1 in) in diameter. Like the rest of the alimentary tract, the oesophagus is made up of four layers—a lining of mucous membrane to enable food to pass down easily, a submucous layer to hold it in place, a relatively thick layer of muscle consisting of both circular and longitudinal fibres, and finally an outer protective covering.

Function

When food enters the mouth it is chewed up by the teeth and lubricated by saliva into a smooth, slippery mass called a bolus. This bolus enters the oesphagus by the act of swallowing, which is a complex activity involving several different groups of muscles. The muscles of throat or pharynx contract, forcing the food towards the upper end of the oesphagus. At the same time, other throat and face muscles raise the tongue up against the roof of the mouth so that food does not get back into the mouth; they also move the palate upwards to prevent food getting into the space at the back of the nose, and close the epiglottis over the raised larynx so that food cannot get into the trachea and lungs and cut off the oxygen supply. Occasionally the epiglottis is not closed in time and food or liquid does get into the larynx. When this happens the substance swallowed is immediately expelled by

forceful coughing—the sensation we know as 'food going down the wrong way'

The first part of swallowing is a voluntary act over which we have conscious control. Once the food has passed the back

This X-ray shows the amazing Stromboli swallowing a sword. He keeps his epiglottis open to allow the sword into his oesophagus without swallowing.

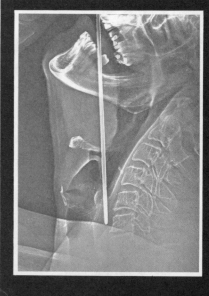

of the tongue, however, the continuation of the act of swallowing is an involuntary, automatic act.

The bolus of food does not just slide down the oesophagus into the stomach, it is actively pushed down by a series of wave-like muscular contractions—a process called peristalsis. The passage of food is, therefore, an active process and not just a passive mechanism depending on gravity; which is why we can eat and drink, if we want to, just as well standing on our heads as sitting down.

Common problems and treatment
A surprising variety of things can pass down the oesophagus without damaging it. People have even been known to swallow broken glass without coming to

Hiatus hernia and the oesophagus

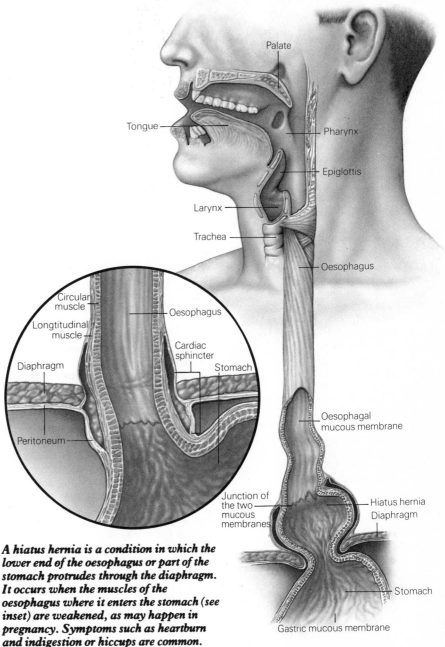

Palate

Tongue

Pharynx

Epiglottis

Larynx

Trachea

Oesophagus

Circular muscle

Longtitudinal muscle

Oesophagus

Cardiac sphincter

Diaphragm

Stomach

Peritoneum

Oesophagal mucous membrane

Junction of the two mucous membranes

Hiatus hernia
Diaphragm

Stomach

Gastric mucous membrane

Frank Kennard

A hiatus hernia is a condition in which the lower end of the oesophagus or part of the stomach protrudes through the diaphragm. It occurs when the muscles of the oesophagus where it enters the stomach (see inset) are weakened, as may happen in pregnancy. Symptoms such as heartburn and indigestion or hiccups are common.

any harm. But, sometimes, if the object swallowed is large enough, for instance if a young child swallows a small toy, then the oesophagus may become blocked. If this happens, swallowed food will be rapidly brought back, the person will retch persistently and will experience pain behind the breastbone. Surgery will be necessary to remove the blockage. Likewise, if a person swallows a corrosive substance, such as acid or strong alkalis like bleach the damage done to the oesophagus can be very serious and may

require surgery to correct it.

Perhaps the most common of all problems in this area is inflammation of the oesophagus (oesophagitis). This is usually caused by acid coming up from the stomach and results in a burning feeling behind the breastbone after eating. This condition, known as 'heartburn', occurs frequently in pregnancy, and is a common symptom of a hiatus hernia. Treatment of oesophagitis normally depends on antacids and drugs to reduce stomach acid.

Oestrogen

Q I have been taking the Pill for a number of years. Will this upset my sex hormones?

A In some women the Pill does upset the normal oestrogen and progesterone levels and this is probably responsible for the side-effects such as cramp, headaches, changes of mood and fluid retention that some women experience. These side-effects usually disappear when the Pill is discontinued. In a few women, the natural cycle is disturbed so much that periods cease and it can be difficult to get them re-started. Fertility, although obviously interfered with by the Pill, usually returns when it is stopped. There are, however, a few women who find it difficult to become pregnant after taking oral contraceptives for a long time.

Q I am just beginning the change of life. Will the lack of oestrogen in my body cause any physical differences?

A The most obvious difference is the cessation of periods. There are also changes in the breasts, which tend to become smaller and less firm. In some women there are also effects on the vagina, which may become less readily moist and supple. This situation can be substantially improved by taking synthetic oestrogen.

Q Does oestrogen have any effect on pregnancy?

A After having stimulated the womb to prepare for a possible pregnancy, oestrogens continue to play an important part in the subsequent pattern of events, though another hormone, progesterone, also has a vital role. Certainly, levels of oestrogen increase throughout pregnancy, reaching a peak just before birth, but rapidly dropping to normal levels immediately after it. Much of this oestrogen is probably manufactured in the placenta rather than in the ovaries. Oestrogen does not seem to play a part in the onset of labour, but it is likely that the high levels of oestrogen during pregnancy keep the enlarging breasts inactive until the time arrives for milk production.

Oestrogen is a general term for a group of female sex hormones, all with slightly different names such as oestrone or oestrol, and all performing an essential function in a woman's reproductive life.

Oestrogens first achieve prominence in a woman's life at puberty. About four years before a girl has her first period (see Menarche, pp 1160-61) the hypothalamus in the brain begins to secrete substances called releasing factors. These act on the pituitary gland and stimulate it to produce the hormones responsible for a girl's sexual development. One is a growth hormone, two others—follicle-stimulating hormone (FSH) and luteinizing hormone (LH)—are responsible for controlling the various changes in the monthly menstrual cycle.

FSH has the effect of stimulating the growth to maturity of egg follicles in the ovary—all of which have been present since before birth. Only a few follicles grow at first, but as they do the layers of cells surrounding them begin to secrete oestrogen. These follicles produce oestrogen for about a month and then fade away. But each month more and more follicles are stimulated by FSH until eventually between 12 and 20 become active at a time. There is thus a gradual increase in the amount of oestrogen circulating in the body, and it is this that triggers the specific changes which we associate with puberty.

Effects of oestrogen

As the months pass, the amount of oestrogen circulating in the body increases more rapidly and this has the effect of stimulating growth in the lining of the uterus, the endometrium, in preparation for its role of accommodating a fetus. Feedback to the pituitary results in it secreting less FSH with the effect that the ovaries in turn produce less oestrogen. Oestrogen support for the thickening of the lining of the uterus is thus withdrawn and it begins to break through the vagina as a mixture of blood and debris—the first 'period' (menstruation). During the period the hypothalamus again stimulates the pituitary to produce more FSH which triggers the ovary to mature another batch of egg follicles and manufacture more oestrogen; and so the cycle is repeated.

The amount of oestrogen rises steadily all through the first or proliferative phase of the menstrual cycle—during which the lining of the uterus is growing thicker until by the 13th day after the onset of the last period the lining is six times its original level. Feedback to the hypothalamus and pituitary causes a slowing down in the production of FSH once the oestrogen peak has been reached, but also stimulates the manufacture of the other major pituitary sex hormone—luteinizing hormone. This also acts on the ovary, stimulating one of the egg follicles to break open and release its egg which then makes its way into the Fallopian tube where it is available for fertilization. Once this monthly cycle is established, it continues until the menopause or change of life.

Oestrogens are necessary not only to initiate puberty and the succession of menstrual cycles but to maintain the woman's other sexual characteristics. If, for any reason, the supply of oestrogen fails, not only do periods cease and fertility fall, but the woman may begin to take on what appears to be a more masculine appearance.

The activity of the hypothalamus, which is the initiator of the chain of events that results in oestrogen production can be influenced by emotional factors and it is in this way that anxiety and depression can affect oestrogen secretion and thus both fertility and menstruation.

Uses of oestrogen

Taking a small daily dose of synthetic oestrogen—hormone replacement therapy (HRT)—as a substitute for what the ovaries are no longer producing naturally, can do much to alleviate the effects of the menopause. Sudden discontinuance of such treatment will bring about an artificial menstruation often called withdrawal bleeding. This technique is sometimes used to provoke regular periods in patients where periods are either erratic or absent. One of the changes that sometimes accompanies the menopause is a drying up of vaginal secretions and this situation can often be improved by the use of oestrogen preparations which must be prescribed by your doctor.

Most oestrogen preparations taken nowadays are chemically manufactured rather than being prepared from natural sources. The most widespread use of these preparations is as a constituent of the contraceptive pill.

Oestrogen production and the developing egg

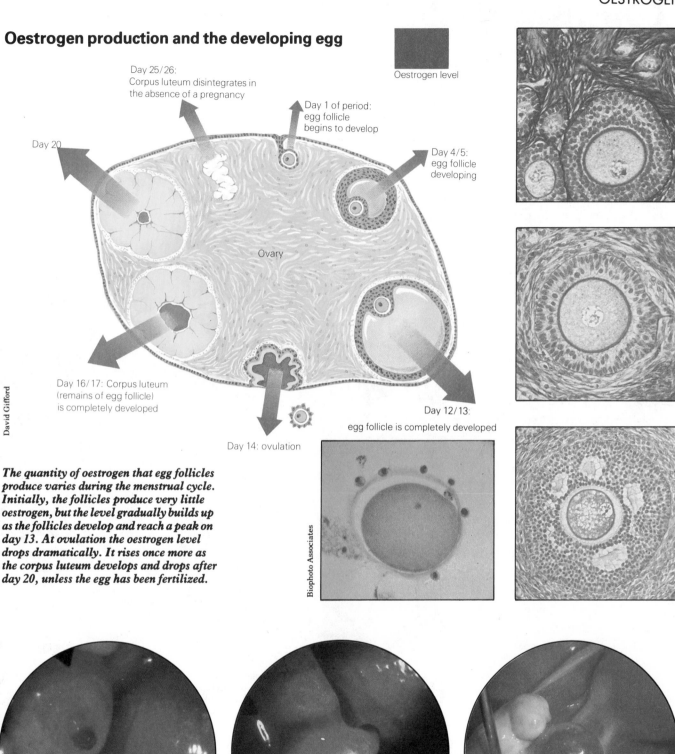

Oestrogen level

Day 25/26:
Corpus luteum disintegrates in
the absence of a pregnancy

Day 1 of period:
egg follicle
begins to develop

Day 4/5:
egg follicle
developing

Day 20

Ovary

David Gifford

Day 16/17: Corpus luteum
(remains of egg follicle)
is completely developed

Day 14: ovulation

Day 12/13:
egg follicle is completely developed

Biophoto Associates

The quantity of oestrogen that egg follicles produce varies during the menstrual cycle. Initially, the follicles produce very little oestrogen, but the level gradually builds up as the follicles develop and reach a peak on day 13. At ovulation the oestrogen level drops dramatically. It rises once more as the corpus luteum develops and drops after day 20, unless the egg has been fertilized.

Dr Med. H. Frangenheim

The egg is just beginning to leave the Graafian follicle in which it has been maturing for at least 10 to 14 days.

The egg is expelled from the ovary towards the Fallopian tube. It is surrounded by a jelly-like fluid from the follicle.

Here artificial hormones have been used to stimulate ovulation. The egg can be seen lying on a small follicular cyst.

Ointments

Q Should I put ointment on a burn?

A After you have cooled down the heat of a burn with cold water, leave it to heal naturally, exposed to the air. If this is impractical, you can use an antiseptic ointment and dressing. The problem is that soothing ointments tend to keep the burn soggy and can bury infection in it, making subsequent cleaning harder. (The same objections apply to the use of ointments on cuts and scratches.)

Q What is the difference between ointment and cream?

A Ointments are greasy substances which can take up water to a certain extent. Creams already have water mixed into them as an emulsion. This means that a cream is cooler, easier to spread and stays on better. Many ingredients will dissolve in oil or water but not both, so creams are the usual vehicle for water-soluble substances. They are stiffer to spread and stay on better. Where either water or oil can be used, ointments work better for thick tough skin (in psoriasis, for example). Creams, such as those used in cosmetics, are much more suitable for sensitive and soft areas like the face.

Q Is it safe to use ointments while I am pregnant?

A A small amount of the active ingredients of any ointment are absorbed through the skin into the body. If the ointment is being used only in a small area, this is no problem, and it is quite safe to continue using it throughout a pregnancy.

However, if you have to use the ointment on the whole body, because of a skin disease, an appreciable amount may be absorbed. You should ask your doctor's advice and may perhaps need a change of medication while you are pregnant. Fortunately, many skin problems improve during pregnancy anyway, and ointments recommended for stretch marks and itching are completely safe to use.

Whether they soothe or soften, protect or heal, ointments are grease-based preparations that cater for a vast range of medical conditions and bodily needs.

An ointment is a greasy preparation for use on the body. It is generally applied to the skin, but special formulations are made for the eyes, mouth and other specific parts of the body. An ointment can be therapeutic (healing) in itself, working in a protective way, or it may have an active ingredient dissolved in it, in which case it is said to be a 'vehicle' for the dissolved drug.

What are ointments?

Ointments are basically greasy substances which can be spread over the skin. There are several types, varying according to the ease with which they can be mixed with water.

Non-emulsifying ointments, such as paraffin, are completely immiscible (unable to be mixed) with water. This means they can be used as barriers to

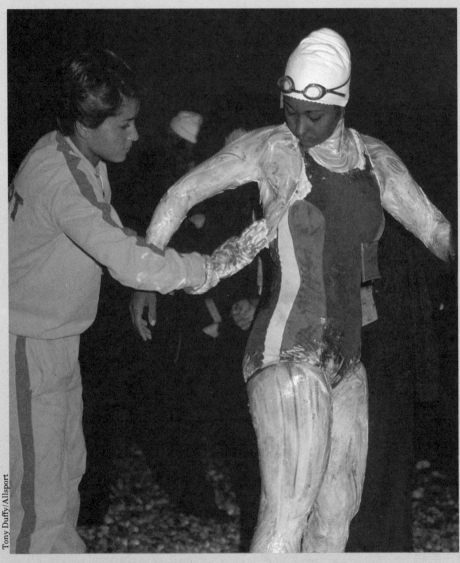

Tony Duffy/Allsport

Some ointments protect the skin from damage by water and wind. Because they are grease-based they stay in place for a considerable time, acting as a barrier between the skin and the outside world, so that it keeps its natural moisture.

prevent the skin becoming wet or, conversely, from drying out. They are helpful, for example, where urine is irritating the skin in an incontinent old person or a baby. Similarly, if the skin is being exposed to extremes of weather, a non-emulsifying ointment is a useful protection.

Emulsifying ointment, on the other hand, contains fats which can dissolve in water into tiny globules. This means that, while retaining its greasiness, emulsifying ointment can be mixed with watery ingredients, and can absorb moisture from the skin. It can therefore be used as a soap substitute and as such is recommended for people who have a dry skin, which will only be made dryer by washing with ordinary soap and water.

The invention of water-soluble ointments has extended the range still further. These are good vehicles for drugs needing an oily base, but can still be easily removed by washing.

Uses of ointments

Ointments can be used simply for their protective properties—as they are by cross-Channel swimmers, for example, who cover themselves in grease before setting off. They are also used as a barrier by yachtsmen, whose hands and faces get very chapped by wind and sea, and by people with dry skin complaints, such as eczema and psoriasis. In these cases, the dry horny skin also needs softening, and the ointments work by preventing natural evaporation, so that the skin is softened by its own moisture. Barrier ointments can also be used to protect normal skin from other harmful substances—wart paint, for example.

The water-resistant properties of ointments make them useful for the eye, mouth, vagina and rectum. In all these moist areas they are able to stay in place better than creams or other preparations,

Avoiding problems

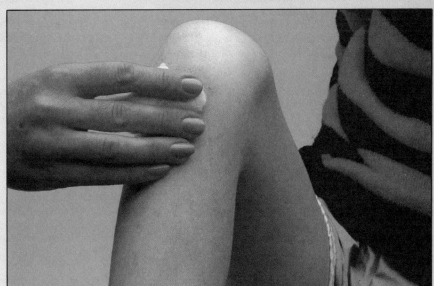

● Clean a wound such as a graze thoroughly, working gently from the centre outwards with a mild antiseptic solution—hydrogen peroxide, for example. If the wound is gritty, scrub it very gently in cold running water to get rid of the dirt. After this, leave it open. Do not cover it with a layer of ointment, as this could seal in any remaining dirt and germs and so cause infection.

● If your eyes are sore, inflamed or itchy, it is important to consult your doctor. Do not try to treat the problem yourself with a proprietary eye ointment obtained from the drugstore.

● If sore or damaged skin does not heal quickly, ask your doctor's advice. Do not keep applying antiseptic ointment to it: it can delay healing.

Steve Bielschowsky

and so do not have to be re-applied so frequently. However, the difficulty in removing them may be a disadvantage in other parts of the body.

As well as being protective, ointments may be used as vehicles for drugs and other active ingredients. The chemicals are simply dissolved in them in the right concentration. They make good bases because most drugs dissolve easily in oily fats, and since ointments mix well with the skin's own greases, their healing properties get right to the skin cells. In pastes, a variation of ointments, a powder is suspended without being dissolved, but here again the ointment will still mix into the skin's own greasy layer, taking the active chemicals to the skin cells where they are to act.

Q I have been using a prescribed ointment for the last three days, but the area of skin seems to be getting more inflamed. Why is this?

A It sounds as if you may be particularly sensitive to some constituent in the ointment. You should stop using it and consult your doctor as soon as possible.

Q When I recently cut my finger I put some old ointment on the wound, and now the cut is going septic. How could this happen?

A There are several important points to be made here. The first is that if the ointment was made up several years ago, it may have lost potency or even changed into substances which would actually inflame your skin. So it is a good thing not to use skin preparations that are over a year old without checking with your doctor or pharmacist first.

The second point is that there are always risks in using a skin preparation which was prescribed previously for one specific condition.

The third point about using an ointment for cuts and grazes is that if they are very thick in consistency and do not actually contain a suitable antiseptic they may seal in the bacteria so that infection is virtually guaranteed. It is safer to avoid using ointments on cuts altogether.

Q My doctor has prescribed an ointment for me which contains a steroid, but because of what I've read and heard about the dangers of steroids, I am very nervous of using the ointment. Are my fears justified?

A Certainly, great care needs to be exercised in using steroid ointments and creams, although they do achieve startlingly successful results in certain conditions.

What is important is to use only very small amounts, spread very thinly over the area concerned. It is also important not to get into the habit of using it on a regular daily basis, but only for a few days at a time. The amount of steroid in such ointments is extremely small and very little is absorbed through the skin.

Ointments for the home

Burns:	Most ointments contain antiseptic (aminacrine hydrochloride) and can be used on a minor second-degree burn—a burn which has blistered. If the burn area does not heal quickly, ask your doctor's advice without delay.
Chilblains:	Chilblain ointment may help to increase blood flow to the skin and the act of actually rubbing it on to the skin may also help to stimulate circulation. However, the best treatment is prevention by keeping the feet and hands warm.
Eye problems:	Eye ointment should be used exactly as the instructions recommend and only for a very short time. If the symptoms persist for several days, ask your doctor's advice.
Skin disorders:	Calamine ointment soothes uncomfortable itchy skin. A protective ointment eases the discomfort of skin made dry and sore by sun or wind. It is also a useful treatment for mild diaper rash.
Stings:	Calamine ointment cools and soothes.
Sunburn:	Calamine ointment and zinc ointment are both soothing.

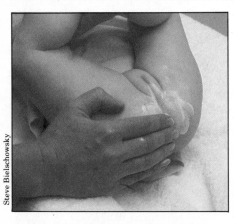

Steve Bielschowsky

A protective ointment has a soothing effect on skin made sore by diaper rash.

Skin diseases have many parallels with diseases of the rest of the body, and can be tackled with the same drug. There are ointments containing all the major drug types: antibiotics for treating skin infections, antihistamines for allergic problems, steroids to reduce inflammation, and so on.

Because of their drug content, these kinds of ointment may require a prescription, but many others are available at the chemist. In particular, there are soothing preparations to rub on injuries. Most of the benefit from them comes from the actual rubbing into the skin, which provides a counter-stimulus to the nerves transmitting pain. This may be intensified by an irritant in the preparation itself which keeps up the stimulus, and encourages bloodflow to the area, so that it gets hot.

Some ointment contains an antiseptic.

Unfortunately, people often think that if they apply it to a wound it will stay free of infection, failing to realize that this will not work unless the wound is clean to start with. If it is not, the end result is a dirty wound covered by a protective layer of ointment which simply seals in the germs so that a serious infection erupts. The wound should be cleaned and left open for any further dirt and infection to come out; it should not be sealed over by ointments, even if they do claim to be antiseptic.

There are large numbers of ointments available for cosmetic purposes. On the whole these are working as barriers, and the other ingredients are merely perfumes and colourings.

Dangers

It is easy to see whether an ointment is causing local problems. The trouble is infection caused by an ointment which is harbouring germs being rubbed into the skin. Always make sure that the skin is clean before applying, and do not seal ointment over broken skin. Occasionally an allergy may develop to an active ingredient or even to the ointment base: this is particularly likely with antihistamine and antibiotic ointments, and it causes a red itchy inflammation of the treated area.

Absorption of drugs through the skin can occur, but usually the dosage is very low. However, problems may occur when large areas of skin are being treated, as they are in eczema and psoriasis, for example. In such cases, never use ointments stronger than necessary to control the skin ailment.

Old age

Q My husband and I are thinking of retiring to the country. Is this a wise move?

A Think carefully before you leave your friends—it's not always easy to make new ones as one gets older. And don't forget that while the country may be fine in summer, you may find yourselves very isolated in winter. Don't rush such an important decision.

Q Since I was a girl I have always taken pride in my appearance. How can I remain looking good now that I'm in my sixties?

A You probably don't need to be told that a sensible diet, high in protein, and regular daily exercise are the best safeguards for good looks as well as good health in the advancing years. Beauty measures could include making sure to oil your skin, especially the lower leg area which becomes very prone to dryness, after a bath. Use a cleansing cream rather than soap on your face and keep make-up light. Don't forget to cream your hands as these become dry, too. Try not to strain your hair with too many combs and pins—this could lead to hair loss. And remember that lots of interests add sparkle to the eye and lightness to the foot.

Q My father, a fit and active 80-year-old, is coming to live with my husband, myself and our three children. We are all very fond of him but wonder if there are any pitfalls?

A If he can have his own room with some of his own furniture, you will probably find that your father will settle in well. At any age it's nice to have even a small place to call one's own. Encourage him to keep active by joining in local activities for old people. And if everyone helps round the house, there is no reason why grandpa shouldn't too—he may be slow at doing the washing-up but he'll feel more useful if he has his own chores like everyone else. Let him take part in family decision-making and, finally, don't fuss him too much—if he wants to retire to his own room to be alone for a while, do respect his wishes.

What is the secret of a satisfying old age? It is not simply luck, but more a combination of an active mind in a healthy body. Older people can do a great deal to help themselves achieve this satisfactory state.

The old saying runs that 'A man is as young as he feels and a woman is as old as she looks'. Many glamorous grandmothers and sprightly grandfathers will testify to the truth of this adage. For old age need not be filled with loneliness, depression and illness—though, unfortunately, this can happen—but it can be a time of constructive leisure, new interests and mature reflection.

Nowadays many people reach retirement with 20 active years ahead of them and society has responded by providing more outlets for the elderly. More and more people are taking their pre-retirement skills to voluntary organizations and even part-time paid jobs, and are remaining active outside the home well into their seventies. Special holidays cater for the senior citizen and increasingly people are taking advantage of them. Many people take up a new hobby on retirement—it can be something as energetic as climbing or as absorbing as gardening. Some people, especially men, take a new interest in their homes and become DIY experts. Should they wish to take advantage of them, most elderly people in towns are well supplied with clubs and day centres nearby which provide interest, activities and companionship.

Natural processes
Certain physical changes do take place in the body as it grows older but this does not mean that old age has to be a time of

Special holidays for older people offer the chance not only to see new places but also to make new friends in the same age group— with a boost to health thrown in.

Picturepoint

later. This means that bones become more fragile and can be broken more easily. Because the bones most affected are the vertebrae, we tend to lose stature and this is the more likely because the discs between the vertebrae tend to shrink, too. Vitamin D (see page 347) helps to prevent bones softening.

Some people in later life have permanently enlarged joints, particularly the knee and wrist. This is not painful and usually does not cause any inconvenience. But any enlargement and any pain in the joints should be reported to

Retirement need not mean a narrowing of horizons. Many older people use their new-found leisure to travel abroad, like this couple (left) sunning themselves on the Greek island of Corfu.

Cycling (below) is an excellent form of exercise—even if few people, young or old, are so enterprising in their choice of machine! Regardless of age, try to keep active – for pleasure as well as for health.

continuous illness. There are various sensible precautions to take, the first of which is to ask your doctor for a check-up when you reach retirement. He can tell you if there are any measures you can take to keep yourself fit—or fitter. Remember, too, to report any odd symptoms or unusual aches and pains to your doctor—don't just put them down to advancing years. It is not bothering your doctor unnecessarily—it is always easier to treat an illness in its early stages.

Knowing what to expect of your body also helps. The following outline of the ageing process is only a guide as people age differently, and different parts of the body age at different times. And everyone knows of a senior citizen of 80 who has all his or her faculties and who is healthier than many an individual at 60. So while there are general guidelines, there is no one pattern for old age.

The muscle of the heart weakens naturally with increasing age, and the arteries harden. This does not mean that exercise should be discontinued—indeed regular exercise can help to keep the heart healthy. But sudden exertion should be avoided, like running for a bus. Any breathlessness or pain in the chest should be reported to your doctor.

As we age, our bones become thinner and lighter. In women, the process starts at about 50 and in men about 10 years

J. Allen Cash Ltd

your doctor. Pain in the joints of an older person may be due to one of the many forms of arthritis, so the sooner it is diagnosed and treated the better.

The most important and noticeable change in the skin is that it becomes drier and wrinkles form. Some people go grey in their thirties while others keep their hair colour until advanced age. Baldness in men is irreversible and women may experience some thinning of the hairs.

Eyes need to be checked annually in later years as after the age of about 45 the lens becomes less flexible and loses some of its focusing power. There is no reason why older people should not use contact lenses if they wish.

This couple (below) hill-walking in the north of England prove that advancing years need not prevent anyone from taking up an energetic open-air pastime.

Any deterioration of the sight or hearing should be reported immediately to your doctor. We tend to take our sight and hearing for granted so that we do not realize how isolated we could feel at its loss or impairment. Often early treatment can improve matters considerably.

Mobility is a vital matter in old age and even if your feet and legs have given you no trouble during your life, it is important to care for them in later years. Some old people who thought themselves crippled have found they could walk easily again after a visit to a chiropodist. Comfortable and supporting shoes are better than wearing bedroom slippers indoors. Any swelling of the ankles or pain in the legs should be discussed with your doctor.

Health in later life
The importance of exercise cannot be over-emphasized. Regular walking, or swimming if you can manage it, is excellent. Exercise helps the circulation and tones the muscles. It is vital to keep the body working properly and there is no reason why you should not be healthy until quite late in life. So long as you wrap up well, there is no reason why you should not take your regular walk in winter too. Even those who are housebound or chairbound can do gentle exercises. If these have been prescribed by a physiotherapist, it is most important that you make an effort and follow their instructions.

Q I'm nearing 75 and while I can manage on my own as yet, I foresee the time coming when I shall need to be looked after. My daughter wants me to live with her and her family but I've seen so many marriages put at risk by an old person that I want to go into a home. There's a nice church home near me—how do I go about applying?

A What a sensitive and thoughtful decision of yours to go into a home when the time comes. You could ring the matron of the home and ask her how you put your name on the waiting list—explain that you don't need a place immediately. Ask her, too, if it would be possible for you to come and visit the home one day: that way you will be sure it's to your liking. Many of today's homes for older people are very pleasant places indeed. You will not regret your decision.

Q My wife and I are in our sixties and I still enjoy making love, but my wife says 'we should be past that sort of thing'. Is she right?

A No. It is both natural and healthy to make love well into old age. It may be that your wife is finding love-making painful due to lack of lubrication of the vagina after the menopause—this can be solved by buying some cream at your local drugstore. If, however, she does feel 'too old', you will have to woo her again. No one is too old for love at 60.

Q My husband retired three years ago and can't seem to adjust. He just sits around the house all day. How can I get him interested in something?

A One wife faced with this situation took a part-time job herself and left her husband to do the housework and cooking—which he did, with great enthusiasm and increasing skill. If you don't think this would work in your case, go to your local hospital and find out what sort of voluntary work they need and try to interest your husband in this.

Another tactic would be to persuade your husband to come along with you to a class, and get him interested in a hobby you could pursue together.

As the years advance it is only too easy to become lazy about getting up, especially if the weather is cold. But this is very bad for the health. Joints get stiff with staying in bed and as each day passes it becomes more difficult to rise. Try to have a routine and get up at a set time each day, even on those rather empty days when it is raining and you don't expect a visitor. Try to find an incentive for getting up each day.

Along with exercise, keeping one's weight down is very important in later life. Obesity puts a strain on all the internal organs, including the heart, and also on the legs and feet. This can mean the risk of illness or immobility. If you are on a fixed income, it is only too easy to indulge a sweet tooth and live on bread and jam and biscuits but it is much better for you if you make the effort and buy cheese, eggs and the easier-to-cook cuts of meat instead. Like exercise, a good diet

Creative artists seldom retire – Pablo Picasso continued to paint into very old age, while his vitality brought him the society of innumerable friends.

demands discipline—but it pays dividends in the long run. Remember that protein and fruit with a little carbohydrate and a small amount of fat is a good recipe for mental as well as physical health—food feeds the brain as well as the body.

Many people reach retirement age having smoked and perhaps drunk heavily since they were young. They see no reason to cut down on their smoking and drinking but it is unfortunately the case that in old age diseases associated with these two habits catch up on us. It is only sensible to cut down on smoking and drinking in the interests of health in later life. Heart and lung diseases are connected with cigarettes and liver disease with drinking.

Mental health

One of the biggest hurdles in life for men, and increasingly for working women, is reaching retirement. Too many people still let retirement come upon them without having made plans for the extra leisure. At first they enjoy staying in bed late and pottering around: then after a

few months they become bored. This is a situation that some companies and trade unions try to avoid by running courses in post-retirement life: anyone who has the opportunity should attend such a course, even if they have their own ideas about what they intend to do. But even if you do not have the chance to attend a special course, try to make real plans for your retirement. Attend evening classes in subjects that interest you before you retire: try to make your life really full before the time comes for you to leave work. Make arrangements to see colleagues after you all leave the firm: explore your local area for clubs to join or ways to get involved with the community.

Don't forget that the solitary occupations like reading and painting are not just an end in themselves: they enrich the mind and make you an interesting conversationalist—a visitor would far rather hear of the progress of your latest

Solitude is not the same as loneliness. Time for yourself, after a lifetime of taking responsibility for others, can be very welcome and refreshing.

Roger Payling

Preparing for a healthy and active old age

● Take regular exercise such as walking and swimming. This will help keep muscles in good tone and improve circulation.
● Keep your weight down. Obesity puts a strain on all the organs.
● Cut down on smoking and drinking as these lead to disease.
● Develop a number of hobbies. This keeps the mind active.
● Keep up with friends old and new. Company keeps you occupied and wards off loneliness and depression.
● Take an interest in current affairs and the younger generation.
● Have your eyes, teeth and feet checked regularly. This could save a lot of bother later.
● Report any unusual symptoms to your doctor. Better an early diagnosis and the chance of successful treatment, than a late discovery and long-drawn out medication.
● Maintain standards of personal hygiene as a daily routine.
● Have your home made safe by the installation of rails, safety fittings, and so on long before you think you will need them.
● Try and do something for others—anything, from joining a local conservation group to baby-sitting. That way you remain a useful part of the community.

painting than all about your back pains. And remember to make your visitors welcome—ask them about their own lives, don't just tell them how hard yours is. Be interested and interesting, in fact.

Many people fear the impairment of faculties that they feel old age inevitably brings. But it need not. The commonest complaint people make is that their memories for recent events is faulty, but even this need not necessarily be the case. What does seem commonly to fail is the ability to learn new tasks easily and the ability to sustain abstract thoughts. But this does not happen overnight and there are many 90-year-olds who appear to keep their mental faculties intact. Probably there is a genetic factor at work here, but anyone who has studied people in older life knows that it is those who take the greatest interest in what is going on around them who remain alert longest.

Nowadays doctors do not look upon confusion as inevitable in old age: it is often caused by illness.

Maintaining independence

Many people who live alone or with a spouse wish to remain independent as long as possible. It is therefore a good idea to make your home as convenient as possible. Make sure that is warm and well-lit. Even if you are on a pension try not to economize on lighting and heating. If you become physically handicapped contact your local social services and ask them if they can provide you with some of the aids, like bathroom grip rails, bath seats or stair rails, which will make moving around your home much easier.

If you or your spouse are finding walking difficult perhaps a stick or a walking frame could make life easier.

Be sure you have a telephone installed. Not only is it invaluable for keeping in touch with friends, but it is essential if you want to summon help. Have a stick which you can bang on the floor or ceiling to alert a neighbour if you need assistance.

Don't be too independent and refuse meals-on-wheels and home helps if you are unable to look after yourself properly. They could make all the difference between remaining in your own home and having to live in some kind of institution.

Don't turn down help if it is offered by neighbours. People like to help and feel useful: do give them that pleasure. Encourage them to come in and chat, too—one can never have too many friends at any age.

One-parent families

Single parenthood is becoming increasingly common. And although parenthood itself may be a pleasure, bringing up children on your own is by no means an easy task.

Q I have recently separated from my husband, and I am worried about the effect on my young children. What should I look out for?

A Your children will need extra reassurance from you, and it is quite normal if they become rather clinging and childish for a while. Schoolwork might deteriorate while the children come to terms with the new situation, so have a word with their teachers. A child who is distressed may begin to wet the bed, throw tantrums or refuse to go to school. If you are worried by your children's behaviour, speak to your doctor or to the local child guidance clinic who may be able to help both you and your children through this difficult stage.

Q I am newly divorced and no longer have the money to spend on nice clothes, toys and treats for my children. What should I do?

A You must explain your new financial situation to your children. Once they understand the reason, they will have to accept things, regardless of whether they like it or not, and perhaps they will develop a more responsible attitude towards money. You will find that good clothes and toys can often be picked up for next to nothing at jumble sales. In any case, your time, love and attention mean far more to your children than expensive treats.

Q I am bringing up two teenage children on my own and have recently taken a full-time job. Should I ask the children to help me with at least some of the housework?

A Certainly. There is no reason why they can't do a moderate amount of housework and shopping—they should be able to fit it in between their schoolwork and other activities. It will encourage their sense of responsibility and independence, as well as taking some of the burden off you. Try to give everyone their own tasks or work out a rota system to avoid arguments occurring.

Few people deliberately choose to bring up children on their own. Usually single parenthood is forced upon them through divorce or death of a partner, and for most people this is a situation for which they are quite unprepared.

Having been used to the convenience of sharing the childcare, financial support and domestic responsibilities, single parents are immediately faced with taking on all the burden themselves.

Moreover they may have to come to terms with a sudden drop in income because even if the absent parent contributes a reasonable amount, there is less money with which to run two households. Often single parents have to find somewhere else to live, and decide whether to get a job or stay at home with the children, or possibly do both.

On top of this they will have to organize a new routine for themselves and their children, and begin to think about creating a new life as a single person.

Unfortunately, much of this has to be done when they feel most vulnerable and insecure. And even when things do sort themselves out, single parents often find the effort to keep on going both physically and emotionally exhausting. However it can be done—as many single parents can attest—often with the help of friends, relatives and one-parent support groups. Indeed single parents find that in time they become more sure of themselves as people, and they discover strengths and abilities which they never knew existed.

Telling the children

There is no one best way to tell a child that you and your partner have decided to separate. Much will depend on individual circumstances and the age of the child.

Generally, though, it is best to give an explanation which is as near to the truth as possible, without going into great detail or apportioning blame. Children

Taking over the other parent's role with a child requires some mental adjustments and the learning of new skills, but in time most single parents cope well.

1396

Roger Payling

must be made to see that they are in no way responsible for the break up, and that both parents love them as much as before. This is particularly true with very young children, who frequently believe that some naughtiness on their part is responsible for the situation, and they need constant reassurance that this is not so. At the same time it is vital that children are made to feel they are loved and valued for their own sakes.

It is often tempting to enlist children on your side against your partner, especially if you have good grounds for feeling ill-treated. But try to remember that in blackening the character of the other parent, you destroy something very important for the child. Your partner may no longer be your partner, but he or she will always be the child's parent. Moreover if children are encouraged to take sides, they will feel guilty about loving the other parent. This can create unnecessary difficulties, lead to renewed tension between parents and generate confusion in children.

What to do with a child during school holidays, when a single parent can't take time off, is a difficulty some parents solve by taking the child to work.

Access

Except in very exceptional circumstances, children will cope better with separation and divorce if they continue to see both parents as well as both parents' families. Unfortunately, this is easier said than done, as access is one issue that generates a great deal of bad feeling.

Visiting arrangements with the other parent can be made happier for the child if parents control any anger and resentment, and allow the child to go off relaxed.

Child access guidelines
- Do not let your anger or resentment towards your partner influence your arrangements
- Organize access so that the partner not living with the children can spend sufficient time with them, ensuring continuity
- Make visits regular, and keep to any timetable you set up
- Never use your visits as an opportunity to spoil the children and win them over to your side
- Organize access so that the children can see both partners' families—cousins, uncles and aunts are important people in children's lives

In the early days especially, the parent who is looking after the child may have trouble coping with visits from the other parent, who may appear less caring and responsible, especially if there have been arguments over money or housing. He or she may raise the argument that the children are upset because the other parent's visits are irregular, or that children are being spoilt by too many treats and are thus harder to handle.

Visiting parents, on the other hand, often feel resentful because they have lost close contact with the child and find the relationship less easy. They may in some cases be angered by the other partner's attitude to having the child stay with them in their new home, possibly with a new partner.

However, the parents must try to come to some agreement and stick to it as far as possible to avoid disappointing the child—for it is the child's interests which must come first. Give and take is needed—regardless of parents' feelings.

Work
One of the first decisions a single parent has to make is whether he or she should work. The advantages are that it gives the single parent a regular income, structure to his or her life, companionship and the chance to renew confidence. The disadvantages are that a parent might find work too physically exhausting on top of other responsibilities, and that it may not even be financially worthwhile. This is particularly true where there are younger children who may need all-day care, which forces the single parent to pay out so much money in help that earnings are exhausted. Finally there is the problem of finding someone reliable, and who is warm and understanding and interested in children.

Working is an individual decision. Try to weigh up what difference the extra money will actually make against your child's needs, and remember that if you do decide to work, your children will require a great deal of undivided attention during the time that they actually spend with you.

Roles
Just as a single parent mother may have difficulties in readjusting to a new job, so a single parent father may find it hard to adapt to a domestic routine, particularly if he is unaccustomed to household tasks.

For all single parents there is the problem of filling the role for the children that their partner once took. It might have been playing sports, comforting children when they're distressed or ill, or dealing with bad behaviour. There may also be difficulties for the single parent of finding the time and enthusiasm for all their children's needs. For this reason the single parent must enlist the aid of friends, neighbours and relatives and offer to reciprocate. Children should also be encouraged to join clubs and take part in out-of-school activities as this will help them widen their interests, and gain confidence by doing different things with new people.

Life of your own
However busy and tired you are as a single parent, you must try to reserve some time for yourself and build a life of your own. This will be difficult at first, but in time it will bear fruit. The more enthusiasm you can bring into the family, the better for you and your children, and the sooner people will stop thinking of you merely as a one-parent family, but rather as a family that is fun to be with.

Roger Payling

Only child

Q When relatives or friends come to see us, our little daughter of three hates them to touch her and doesn't speak at all, not even to their children. What can we do to make her more sociable?

A A good starting-point would be to persuade visitors, very tactfully, not to touch and hug her. Adults tend to overdo this anyway, forgetting that most children dislike it, certainly as they get a little older. Let your little girl do whatever she wants to amuse herself when you have visitors, but if she has friends at play-school arrange for them to visit her at home.

Q My son of seven has an imaginary 'friend' called Robin. He holds long conversations with him, even at mealtimes, and appears to find him quite as real as my husband and me. Is there any danger in this fantasy?

A No. Many children have imaginary friends. If your son has invented Robin, it is because he needs the company of a constant companion as well as that of loving parents. Accept 'Robin', make him welcome, and also encourage your son to make real friends.

Q Our only child – a daughter – is nearly 14, and although she's very attractive and has lots of friends, she often spends her spare time at home, reading or listening to music. We want her to get the best out of life, and are worried that she may be staying at home with us because she feels she ought to. What should we do?

A There doesn't seem to be anything that needs to be done: in fact, your daughter, wise girl, is surely getting the best out of her life. She has loving parents, she has friends, she has interests that give her a great deal of pleasure. She doesn't always need to go out and enjoy herself: she can obviously find a great deal of happiness in staying at home, and the company of her parents contributes to this. Don't spoil the relationship by nagging your daughter to go out.

Only children have advantages and disadvantages. They have their parents' undivided support and attention but it may take them longer to adjust to the company of other children of their own age.

The family is a miniature society. Living with our closest relatives while we are children helps to shape our response to everyone with whom we come into contact throughout the rest of our lives. We become social creatures partly in order to survive. We learn from the example of others, and the learning process begins at a very early age.

Early childhood

For the first months of life, a baby has to be entirely self-centred in order to satisfy the basic needs of food, warmth and sleep. The parents of a young baby understand and accept this, but if they have older children too, they try to share love and attention as equally as possible. As a result, the baby with elder brothers and sisters learns quite early in life that he or she is not the centre of the world after all.

For an only child, this particular lesson may take some time to learn. Where there is no one else to need or compete for the

The only child has the benefit of his parents' undivided love and attention. He need not be spoilt, but he may be precocious.

Ron Sutherland

parents' love and time, the necessary self-centredness of the baby may turn into the destructive selfishness of the 'spoilt' child who is quite ready to compel attention if it is not given freely. If this becomes a set pattern of behaviour, the only child may later find it difficult to make and keep friends, or to sustain close relationships in adult life: his or her expectations of other people will always be unrealistic and, always, ultimately disappointed.

In larger families, brothers and sisters learn, more or less unconsciously, to adapt to one another and to accept the fact that they have to share the world with other people. The only child needs practice in sharing and in acknowledging the rights of others.

A sense of identity

Brothers and sisters help one another—not always gently—to achieve a realistic sense of identity. Children who are used to living together can be extremely outspoken about one another's faults—and even about physical appearance. At the same time, they can also, when necessary, show an absolutely united front to the outside world: all differences and criticisms of each other are forgotten as they suddenly turn into a clan bound together by invincible loyalties.

Until it is time to go to play-school or nursery, the only child may have almost no experience in dealing with other children as rivals, allies or friends. This is a disadvantage, but to balance it, the child probably has the capacity to enjoy the company of adults. The child whose emotional world is secure, who knows without question that he has the complete love and support of his parents is likely to be optimistic and self-confident—and sometimes precocious and rather conceited. His optimism and confidence will be valuable throughout life, but the self-complacency will arouse antagonism, and so the parents of an only child need to find a way of discouraging it without damaging either the child's sense of identity or his feelings of pleasure in it.

One-child parents

The only child needs other children—and so do his parents. The relationship between a child and an adult can be extraordinarily rewarding for both of them, but it is quite unlike the relationship between child and child, for this has elements in it that no adult, however loving, can provide.

Young children at play very often look and behave like adversaries. They shout, squabble, insult one another, use physical force to express a point of view—their friendships have very little room for civility or affection, but this does not make them any the less real or valuable. One of the main characteristics of human life is conflict: conflict of opinion, of belief, of emotion and will. There are times

Only children often possess a great capacity for enjoying their own company. They can actually accept the solitude that bores others and put it to positive use—as a result, developing their powers of thought and imagination.

when it is painful, but it is also a source of energy and change and so, given the basic design of the human personality, it is necessary. Without it there would be lethargy and stagnation.

The child who grows up with older children discovers quite soon what conflict of interest means, and that one person's freedom necessarily limits another's. The only child whose wishes and rights are always acknowledged may find it hard to understand and accept conflict without apprehension or anger. Parents are able to teach their children many valuable things, but it is children only who can teach one another what opposition really means.

To a child who has had almost nothing but adult company for the first two or three years of life, other children may seem an intrusion, and sometimes a very unwelcome one. The solution is to accustom the only child to the company of his contemporaries from a very early age, as soon as awareness of the outside world begins. Two babies touching, making noises, throwing their teddy bears at one another are beginning to teach one another the rudiments of social life, just as other young animals do, through play.

As well as being a learning process, play is a release of energy for young creatures. Kittens, puppies, small children all show very much the same kind of exuberance, the same pleasure in health and movement for its own sake, when they play together. Only children have just as much vitality and stamina as others, but they need the stimulus of young company to express it. If they lack it, they sometimes become rather pre-occupied with avoiding hurt or discomfort, a characteristic which other children—and some adults—find very irritating.

A child needs other children in order to find out what kind of person he or she is. The parents of an only child generally love him unreservedly and sometimes without much objectivity. The child for his part knows that he has his parents' approval and support, simply because he is who he is. This knowledge gives him great reassurance and comfort, but it may also give him, when he is beginning to grow up, the idea that his personality and conduct need no modification whatsoever, and that anyone who criticizes him is automatically wrong. He will need to modify this attitude as he grows older.

The pleasures of an only child

An only child may well find the companionship of other children difficult to accept and enjoy at first, but on the other hand, he is very likely to enjoy solitude and to feel at ease in his own company. A child who likes to be on his own is by no means lonely or anti-social: on the contrary, the person who can enjoy time spent by himself often learns to value the friendship of others highly.

The parents of an only child are usually wise enough to let him be himself and not to try to mould him to a pattern. In a larger family the child who does not fit in with the rest—the one who wants to read when everyone else has decided to go roller-skating—can sometimes be made to feel an outsider, a nuisance to parents and brothers and sisters alike.

The happiest childhood combines what is best in the life of an only child—the certainty that he has his parents' unswerving love and support—with what a larger family has to give: the companionship, the stimulus and the truthfulness of other children. Only children can find companionship at an early age in a play group and the experience gained can benefit them throughout life.

Open-heart surgery

Q My son has a hole in the heart but they are not going to operate. Why is this?

A There are many types of hole in the heart, but basically the only ones that need treating are the large ones which affect the functioning of the heart. A small one can be of no importance and should not prevent your son from leading a perfectly normal life.

Q My wife has just had an open-heart operation and she was in the intensive care unit for three days afterwards. Does this mean that there were problems?

A No. It is routine for all patients who have had open-heart surgery to go into the intensive care unit for a few days after the operation so that they can have the specialized nursing care that they need.

Q I have been told I need a valve in my heart replaced. Isn't this a rather risky operation?

A In the early days of open-heart surgery there was a high risk involved, but nowadays the risk is small. If you have been told that you need a valve replacement the chances of success are good.

Q Can you tell me what an artificial heart valve is like?

A There are various types but the commonest ones are either a ball of plastic about the size of a small marble which sits inside a metal cage, or else like a little trap door which opens and shuts a small amount. Both types allow blood to flow in one direction only. Sometimes specially prepared pig's heart valves are used instead.

Q What is the most common reason for performing open-heart surgery—and what is the most unusual?

A The commonest reason used to be replacement of a heart valve, but now this has probably been overtaken by coronary artery by-pass surgery. Heart transplantation is the least frequently performed type of open-heart surgery.

Modern heart surgeons can perform operations that were previously unthinkable – like heart transplants, for example – because the patient's heart can now be stopped during surgery and the blood circulated by machine.

The term open-heart surgery is used to describe surgery on the heart when the chest is opened, the function of the heart taken over by a machine, and the heart operated on directly. Before this technique was developed, any operations on the heart were performed through a small incision through which instruments were passed into the heart, and surgery was performed with the heart still beating.

In the 1950s, with the advent of new technology, a machine was devised which could pump the blood without damaging the red blood cells too much, and at the same time saturate the blood with oxygen. This meant that the patient's heart could be allowed to stop beating temporarily, so that operations could be carried out inside it.

Before the operation

Before undergoing open-heart surgery for any type of heart disease, the patient will have had several tests, and will be treated with medicines if at all possible. Surgery will, however, be recommended if the disease does not respond well to treatment. In the early days of open-heart surgery, the patient was often so ill by the time he or she came to have an operation that the results were poor. Nowadays, surgery is recommended much earlier on in the progress of disease when the patient is relatively fit and able to withstand a major operation.

To diagnose the exact nature of the heart disease, all patients will have a cardiac catheterization. A fine tube one millimetre (1/25 in) in diameter is passed into a blood vessel in the arm or leg, and fed into the heart. Pictures can then be taken of the heart and an exact diagnosis made by injecting a special kind of dye which is opaque to X-rays. The tube can also be used to measure blood pressure, and can be passed into the coronary arteries to show up narrowing or a blockage of the arteries.

The operation

The patient is taken to the operating theatre and anaesthetized in the anaesthetic room in the usual way, with an injection followed by gas when the patient is unconscious. Still in the anaesthetic room, the patient will have an intravenous drip (a drip into a vein) together with a needle in an artery and a vein to measure the pressure in the artery and vein during and after the operation.

The patient is then taken into the operating theatre and the operation itself is begun. First of all, the skin over the sternum (breastbone) is cut, and then the sternum itself is divided using an electric saw. The division is widened with special instruments called retractors, and the heart is then exposed.

The next step involves transferring the patient on to the by-pass machine, and this is obviously a step which has to be performed very carefully. Otherwise, serious damage to the brain could result. During this stage, the pressure in the arteries is continuously monitored on a television screen.

First, a large tube is inserted into the aorta (the main artery leading out of the heart) and another one is inserted into the vena cava (the main vein bringing blood back to the heart). These tubes are connected up to the by-pass machine, which consists of a pump and an oxygenator: this is a membrane system through which the blood flows before going back into the patient.

The machine is looked after by a highly trained technician who monitors the pressure of the blood and the speed of

Specialist nursing care after open-heart surgery includes continuously monitoring the patient's heart on a machine.

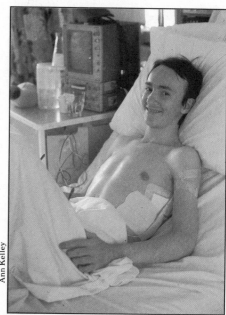

Ann Kelley

The function of the by-pass machine

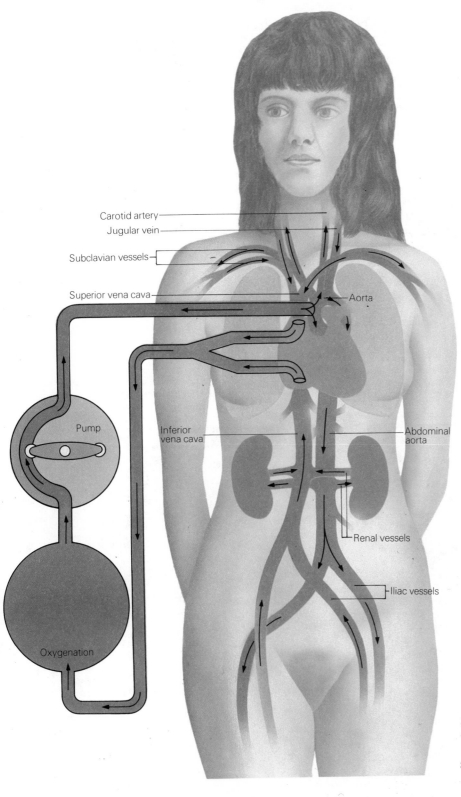

Carotid artery
Jugular vein
Subclavian vessels
Superior vena cava
Aorta
Pump
Inferior vena cava
Abdominal aorta
Oxygenation
Renal vessels
Iliac vessels

flow. Thus the blood comes out of the patient from the vena cava, along a tube to the by-pass machine, through the machine, and back into the patient via another tube. The patient's heart, which is now empty, usually stops spontaneously, or can be stopped by an electric shock or special drugs. From now on the heart can be operated on as its function has been taken over by the by-pass machine.

Different operations

In a hole in the heart operation, a cut is made through the muscle of the heart to reveal the defect. This is repaired sometimes by sewing the edges of the hole together, or sometimes by sewing a patch of artificial material or a portion of the heart's fibrous covering—the pericardium—over the defect. The cut in the heart is then sewn up.

There are four valves in the heart and their function is to allow blood to flow in one direction only, so that when the heart contracts blood is forced out into the arteries, and when the heart relaxes more blood enters the heart from the veins. The valves can become faulty either by becoming leaky so that blood can pass in both directions, or by becoming constricted so that blood has difficulty in passing through them.

In a valve replacement operation the old valve is cut out and a new one is sewn in position. Replacement valves are either made from metal and plastic, or a specially prepared natural valve from a pig's heart is used. They are sewn in place with many fine stitches, to ensure that there is no leak between the valve and the heart muscle.

Coronary arteries can become narrowed and when they do the blood supply to a particular part of the heart becomes inadequate. If this happens suddenly, the patient has a heart attack; but if it happens gradually, the patient suffers from angina. If a coronary arteriogram (X-ray of the coronary arteries) shows a localized blockage, then surgery may be desirable.

In coronary artery surgery the commonest procedure is a coronary artery by-pass graft. Here, the blockage is by-passed using a piece of vein. First of all, a length of vein is taken from the patient's own leg, and it is cut to the right length. Then two small holes are made in the diseased coronary artery, one above and one below the blockage. The vein is then sewn onto the holes using tiny stitches, so that one end of the vein is above, and one end below the blockage. This type of surgery has become much more common in the past few years, and is most often performed on patients with severe chest pain which comes on after exertion.

Open-heart surgery is made feasible by the use of a heart-lung by-pass machine which temporarily takes over the heart's function. Two tubes are inserted into the patient, one into the aorta and one into the vena cavae. These are connected to the by-pass machine which takes over the pumping and oxygenating of the blood.

Open-heart surgery (above) is carried out by a highly skilled team. The by-pass machine can be seen on the left. A neat scar (right) is all there is to show.

This applies especially to people with valve disease, and to children born with heart defects. In the days before operations for hole in the heart, if the defect was a serious one there was very little chance of many of these children surviving into adulthood.

The statistics for operations for coronary artery disease are not so well evaluated, because surgery for coronary artery disease has not been performed for so long. However, there is a lot of evidence to suggest that coronary artery surgery does prolong life in many cases.

It is probably fair to say that the outlook after the operation depends very much on the medical care given before the operation—assuming that the operation goes well and with no complications. The risks of surgery nowadays are so much smaller that the outlook may well be determined by how long the patient had the heart disease before seeking medical help.

However, if the condition is diagnosed in good time and an operation is performed, the long-term outlook is extremely good. Many people with artificial valves can lead near normal lives.

With the heart stopped from beating, the surgeon can perform complex and delicate surgery on the tissues.

After the operation

When the operation on the heart has been performed, the patient has to be taken off the by-pass machine and the heart restarted. This is done by stimulating the heart electrically, and gradually phasing out the by-pass machine, at the same time monitoring the arterial pressure carefully. Sometimes drugs have to be injected into the heart to persuade it to contract forcefully.

A fine wire is left in the muscle of the heart, coming out through the chest wall, so that if the heart starts beating irregularly in the immediate postoperative period, the wire can be connected to a pacemaker straight away. The by-pass tubes are removed, and the breastbone is stitched together using wire stitches. Several drainage tubes are usually left in for a few days after the operation, and the arterial and venous pressure monitoring lines are also left in until the patient's condition is stable.

Obviously the time taken to recover from the operation varies with the type of operation and how ill the patient was beforehand, but most people take about three months to convalesce. If an artificial valve is inserted, the patient will be given anticoagulant tablets, to prevent blood clotting on the valve.

Outlook

The advent of open-heart surgery in the 1950s was a major advance in the treatment of many heart conditions. Before these operations came into being, many people died who would have survived for many years if they had been operated on.

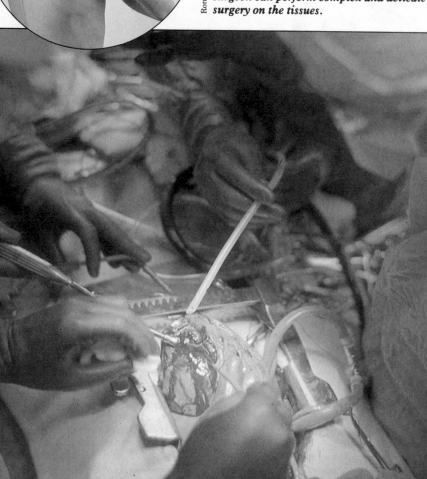

Operating theatre

Q Who are the people in the surgeon's team who actually help with the operation?

A The number of people in the team varies with the size of the operation. For a major operation there will be the surgeon, one or two assistants, and the nursing staff. The assistants are usually surgeons or doctors as well, although they might perhaps be medical students. The operating theatre nurse is the person responsible for getting all the instruments ready for the operation, and handing the appropriate ones to the surgeon.

Q My husband had an operation on his stomach last week, and he was down in the operating theatre for about four hours. Does this mean that the operation went wrong, or was very difficult?

A No, not necessarily. Nowadays, the patient is kept in the recovery room after the operation, until he is more or less awake, before being sent back to his room. There he is looked after by staff trained in this speciality. Your husband may have taken a while to come around from the operation, but this is perfectly normal.

Q Is anything done to reduce the possibility of eye fatigue during long operations?

A The drapes used to cover the area around the operation are usually a restful colour, such as grey or green, and this is where the surgeon will focus his attention. Then, if he has a good theatre nurse helping him, he rarely needs to look up, because the instruments he needs are put into his hand. Moreover, the light which is used does not cast shadows, thus enabling him to see clearly.

Q Could an operation wound become infected nowadays?

A There is a slight possibility of this happening with certain operations, such as appendectomy, but any infection would be treated with antibiotics or a secondary operation, and would cause no serious problems.

Operations were once performed before an audience of surgeons and students. The term 'operating theatre' survives, but has changed radically in meaning, due to modern techniques of sterilization and anaesthesia.

An operating theatre, which is also called an operating suite, is the area in a hospital where patients are prepared for an operation, the operation is carried out, and the patient then recovers before going back to his or her room. Within the same complex are scrubbing-up and preparation rooms where the surgical team gets ready, and where instruments are laid out on special trolleys after being sterilized in the sterilizing unit. Administration of the operating suite is carried out in adjoining offices. In a big hospital, there may be a dozen operating theatres, each with its own operating list.

Sterilization
In the last century it was discovered that infection in a surgical wound could be

The modern operating theatre is well-equipped and as sterile as possible. Lighting is precisely positioned so the surgeon and his assistants have a clear, well-defined field of vision in which to operate.

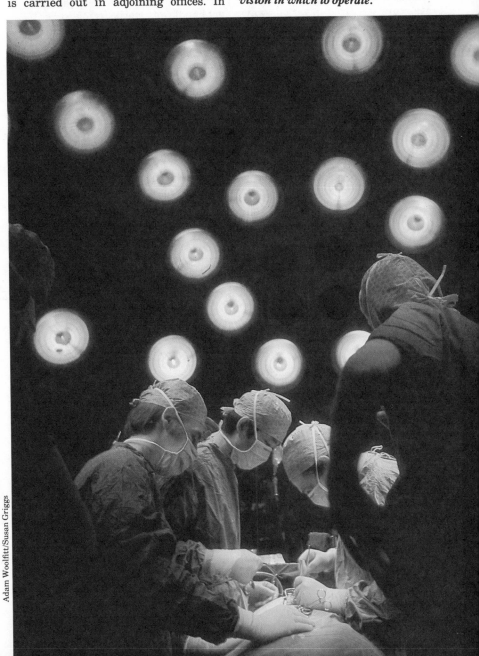

Adam Woolfitt/Susan Griggs

prevented by using certain techniques to destroy bacteria in the air, on the surgeon's hands and on the instruments. Before this, virtually every wound became infected, and a patient was very likely to die from the infection, even if the operation itself was successful. Nowadays wound infection is a very unusual occurrence thanks to modern sterilization methods.

The air in the operating-suite is cleaned through filters which remove bacteria, and is pumped through vents into the theatre itself. The pressure maintained ensures that air is then swept out of the various exits in the whole suite. All the air in the theatre should therefore be clean, and there is no need for an airlock system when entering or leaving the theatre-suite.

All instruments, stitches and anything in contact with the wound during the operation are sterilized in various ways. They may be heated in a device called an autoclave, which is a pressurised chamber capable of delivering superheated steam. Disposable equipment is usually sterilized by gamma-irradiation at the factory, while those instruments which would be damaged by the heating process are chemically disinfected.

Everyone who enters the operating theatre area has to change into special clothes, including shoes. The surgeon and his assistants clean their arms and hands with disinfectant in a process known as 'scrubbing-up', and wear sterile gowns and rubber gloves. All members of the team wear masks to prevent germs being breathed into the wound.

The patient's skin in the area of the proposed operation is disinfected, and once surgery is in progress, nobody except the surgeon and his assistants may touch the operating-field. The surgeon himself must not touch anything that has not been sterilized. There will be, however, several other assistants in the theatre, such as the anaesthetist and nurses, who are free to move about provided they do not handle any sterile items.

The theatre in readiness for the next operation. All this sophisticated equipment is vital for the actual operation – or for any emergency.

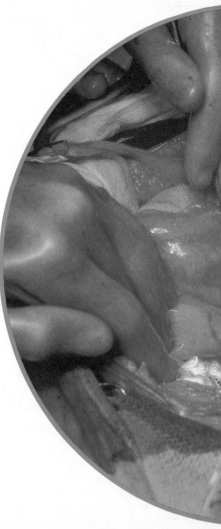

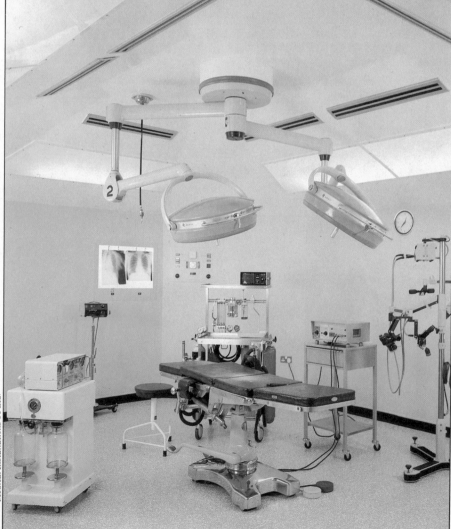

Medical Installations Co Ltd.

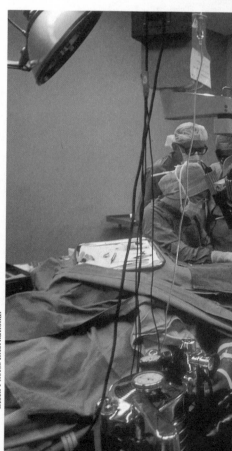

Stock Photos International

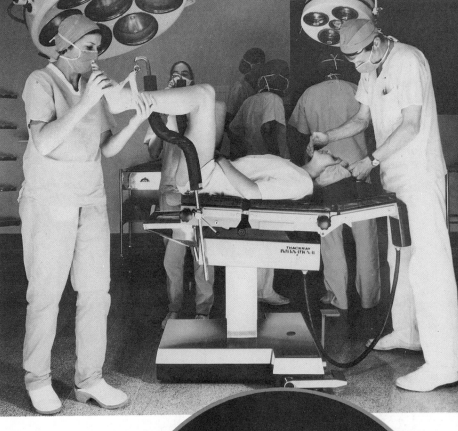

The operating table (above and right) has to be versatile to cope with different surgical positions and to provide adequate support for the patient's body.

Though an operation in progress may look like a crush (left), everyone has specific duties to carry out. The only hands which are allowed in the 'operating-field' (left, above) are those of the surgeon and his assistants.

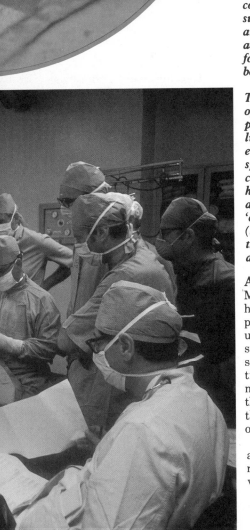

Charles Thackeray

Anaesthesia

Modern anaesthesia requires the use of highly sophisticated equipment. A patient undergoing major surgery usually has an intravenous injection of a substance which puts him to sleep within seconds. This takes place in the anaesthetic room, which is a small room immediately adjoining the operating theatre. The patient is then wheeled into the theatre and is kept asleep, during the operation by gas.

A machine administers the correct amount of gas and oxygen via a tube connected to the windpipe. In many cases a ventilator is also used, which acts as a pump, pushing gas and oxygen in and out of the lungs. This may be necessary since, at the same time as the anaesthetic, the patient may receive a muscle relaxant to make it easier for the surgeon to work, which tends also to affect the muscles of breathing.

Modern developments

Innovations include a sophisticated type of sealed unit with air-locks, used in the theatre itself, and 'space-suits' worn by the surgeons so that none of their expired air reaches the patient. The risk of infection being allowed to develop is thereby reduced even further.

Ophthalmology

Q If I need an operation on my eye, will it be done by an ordinary surgeon, or will it be done by an ophthalmologist?

A In the US and UK, all eye operations are carried out by specialist eye surgeons—ophthalmologists. The ophthalmologist is equipped with special instruments that are used for eye surgery, many of which are scaled down versions of ordinary surgical instruments. Special equipment is also needed to examine the eye in order to make an accurate assessment of the trouble.

Q At what age should children first have their eyes tested?

A One of the main functions of child health clinics is to test eyesight, so all babies should be having their sight tested on a regular basis from the age of six months onwards. One of the most important things that the clinic does is to look for squints so that they can be treated early to avoid the suppression of sight in the affected eye. It is quite normal for babies to have a squint soon after birth, but it should have disappeared by the age of three months. So if you think your baby is still squinting after this age, you should take him or her to your doctor or to the clinic to be looked at. After the child has started school regular checks will probably be made by the school health service.

Q If you are having an ordinary medical, would the doctor check your eyes, or do you have to see an ophthalmologist?

A Most medicals include some assessment of your visual acuity — the ability to see objects without blurring. The doctor will also use an ophthalmoscope to look at the back of the eye (retina) — this is the only place in the body where blood vessels can be seen clearly. If your doctor suspects that you need glasses, he or she will send you to see an optometrist. Or, if he feels that your eyes need to be looked at by someone with more specialist knowledge, you will probably be referred to an ophthalmologist.

Doctors who specialize in ophthalmology are equipped to deal with all aspects of eye disease – and they can perform intricate surgery to save sight.

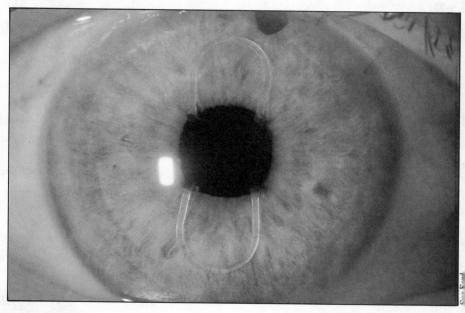

To aid vision, a plastic lens is sometimes implanted into the eye after a cataract has been removed.

Ophthalmology is the study of eye disease. It is an unusual area of medicine as nearly all the doctors who specialize in it are experts in two fields – not only are they eye specialists, but they are also highly-skilled surgeons.

As a specialist, the ophthalmologist carries out complicated tests on the eye, detects problems and prescribes treatment; as a surgeon, he or she performs intricate and delicate operations to improve, and often save, eyesight.

Treating eye problems
Almost all of us have had our eyes tested at some time in our lives, either for glasses or as part of a general medical check-up. But only people with more serious problems will need to go to an ophthalmologist.

If you go to your doctor with some deterioration in your vision, he or she will examine your eyes. If the problem is one of a refractive error (an inability to focus properly), your doctor will advise you to have your eyes tested for glasses by an optometrist. If you need specialized corrective treatment, you may be sent to an ophthalmic practitioner—a doctor who specializes in eye problems but does not do any surgery. Fortunately, however, only a few people will actually be found to have symptoms, like the clouding of vision caused by cataracts (see pp 266-7), that would make referral to an ophthalmologist necessary.

Ophthalmologists also deal with a great many cases of trauma (accidental damage) to the eyes. Despite the eye's vulnerability to certain types of injury, many people fail to wear protective goggles when working with industrial equipment, such as grinding wheels or jackhammers, or even when riding on motorcycles. As a result, ophthalmologists often have to perform quite intricate operations to remove chips and splinters that have penetrated the cornea (the transparent front to the eye) and have lodged in front of the pupil.

Ophthalmic equipment
One of the basic tools of the ophthalmic trade is the ophthalmoscope, which is used by all doctors and optometrists, not just eye specialists. The ophthalmoscope shines a thin pencil of light into the eye and enables the doctor to look along the beam at the retina, the light-sensitive surface at the back of the eye. It also has a number of lenses so that other parts of the eye can be examined.

When a more detailed look at the front of the cornea, the anterior chamber or the iris is needed, an instrument called a slit lamp microscope is used. The ophthalmologist may also instil a little flourescent dye into the eye to make any scratches or abrasions on the cornea show up more clearly. The slit lamp is also used in conjunction with a tenometer to measure the pressure in the eye. Raised pressure is an indication of glaucoma (see page 573).

Eye surgery

Although the ophthalmologist spends a good deal of time in the eye clinic, testing various aspects of people's vision, perhaps the most exciting part of his or her job is in the operating theatre. There are now many operations that are carried out on the eye — all of them requiring great skill and precision. Much of the time, the size of the structures involved is so small that the surgeon uses a special operating microscope.

One of the most common operations that is carried out by eye surgeons is the removal of a cataract. The diseased lens can be surgically replaced by a plastic intraocular lens or by glasses, both of which help to aid vision.

Surgical treatment may also be necessary to prevent loss of sight as a result of glaucoma. By operating on the iris and allowing fluid to drain from the anterior chamber of the eye, the ophthalmologist can relieve the high pressure in the eyeball that is causing poor vision.

When damage to the cornea results in scar formation it may become opaque, making the eye effectively blind. Here again, surgery can help by cutting out the

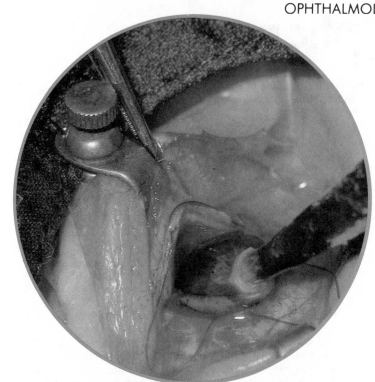

opaque part of the cornea and replacing it with a corneal transplant.

Operations are also carried out on the structure surrounding the eye, such as adjusting the eye muscles in order to correct a squint, and clearing the tear ducts that drain into the nose to treat very watery eyes.

Most cataracts affect the entire lens and need to be removed surgically. One of the methods used involves the use of a cyroprobe (above) – a probe with a frozen tip.

A slit lamp microscope (below) is often used by the ophthalmologist if a more detailed look at the eye is needed.

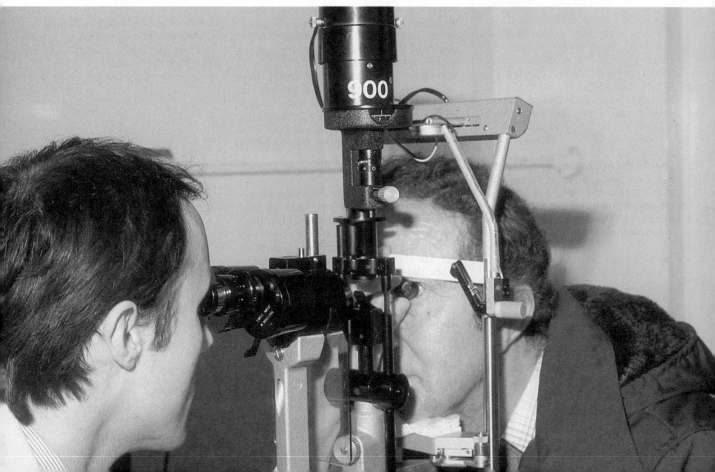

Optic nerve

The optic nerve is a bundle of nerve fibres carrying impulses from the retina – the light-sensitive lining of the eye – to the base of the brain.

Behind the lens of the eye are countless tiny light-sensitive cells which form the coating to the back of the eye, called the retina. Every single cell is connected by a nerve to the brain where information about pattern, colours and shapes is computed. All these nerve fibres collect together at the back of the eye to form one main cable known as the optic nerve. This runs back from the eyeball through a bony tunnel in the skull to emerge inside the skull bone just beneath the brain in the region of the pituitary gland; here it is joined by its fellow optic nerve.

The nerves from each side then cross over so that some information from the left eye is passed to the right side of the brain and vice versa. Nerves from the temporal side of each retina do not cross over and so stay on the same side of the brain whereas those fibres from the part of the eye which does most of the seeing run to either side of the brain.

The optic nerve

The optic nerve is nothing more than a bundle of nerve fibres carrying minute electrical impulses down tiny cables, each of which is insulated from the next by a fatty layer called myelin. At the centre of the main cable is a large artery which runs its entire length. This is known as the central retinal artery. This artery emerges at the back of the eye and the vessels from it spread over the surface of the retina. There is a corresponding vein which runs back down the optic nerve alongside the central retinal artery which drains the retina.

Location

Nerves emerging from the retina are sensory—in other words they do not supply messages to muscle and, unlike nerves supplying muscle (motor neurons) which only have one connection on their way to the brain, optic neurons make more than one connection. The first of these lies just behind the point where the sensory information from each eye is swapped. This cross-over point is known as the optic chiasma and lies very close to the pituitary gland. Immediately behind this cross-over is the first connection or cell station known as the lateral geniculate body. Here, information from left and right is swapped again across the midline. The function of this connection is linked with the reflexes of the pupils.

From the lateral geniculate body the nerves fan out on each side around the temporal (side) part of the brain forming the optic radiation. They turn slightly and collect together to pass through the main exchange, the internal capsule, where all the motor and sensory information supplying the body is concentrated. From there the nerves pass to the back of the brain to the visual cortex.

What the optic nerve does

There are two types of light-sensitive cells in the retina, the rods and the cones, and just like photo-electric cells they convert light energy into electricity. The rods are used principally to make out objects in the dark and they are very sensitive to movement so that they notice objects coming in from the extremes of the visual field in dim light. The cones on the other hand are responsible for sharp colour vision and they are most plentiful at the point where the lens focuses the light, known as the fovea. However they are completely deficient at the point where the optic nerve enters the eye. This

A vertical section through a human eye, showing the optic nerve (below). Closeup of the 'blind spot', the retinal area covered by the optic nerve (bottom).

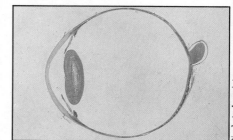

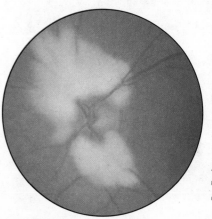

The mechanics of seeing

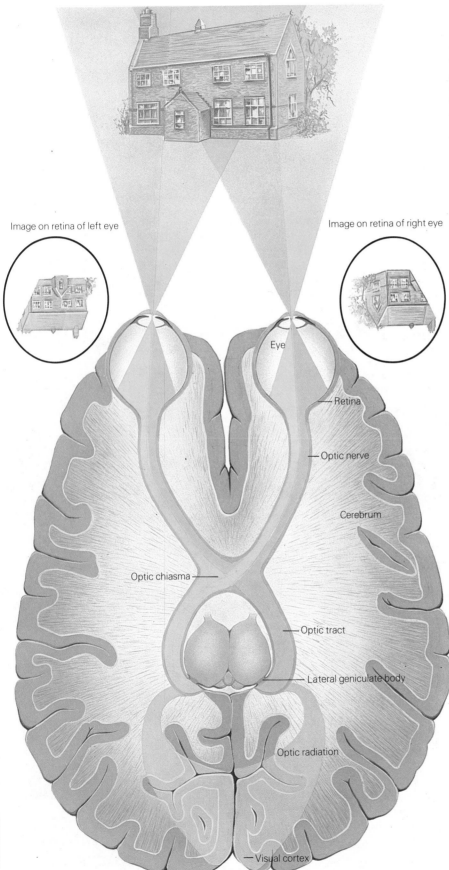

Image on retina of left eye

Image on retina of right eye

Eye

Retina

Optic nerve

Cerebrum

Optic chiasma

Optic tract

Lateral geniculate body

Optic radiation

Visual cortex

Elaine Keenan

is known as the blind spot because light focused here is not perceived.

The diameter of the pupils is controlled in much the same way as the aperture in an expensive camera. Light falling on the retina sends impulses up the optic nerve to the cell station just behind the optic chiasma and then back down, to a motor nerve supplying the muscle of the pupil. The brighter the light the tighter the pupil constricts.

What can go wrong

Obstruction of the central retinal artery leads to sudden total blindness. Fortunately this is rare but may occur if the nerve becomes swollen in its bony tunnel and presses the artery as a result. The blood vessels running over the top of the retina may rupture and bleed over the surface, thereby cutting out the light. This is what often happens to diabetics.

Inflammation of the optic nerve itself is not uncommon during the course of multiple sclerosis. This results in a special kind of visual loss resulting in a blind spot in another part of the retina. This is known as a scotoma. If the optic nerve is sufficiently inflamed it turns pink and sticks out like the head of a drawing pin from the back of the eye, a condition known as papilloedema. Tumours of the pituitary gland may press on the chiasm producing various visual abnormalities depending on what fibres pass beneath at that point. Perhaps the most common tumour to do this is the one causing the glandular condition known as acromegaly.

It is common for a stroke to interfere with the blood supply to the nerves passing through the internal capsule, the main telephone exchange of the brain. Damage here results in complete loss of movement and sensation on one side of the body and inability to see objects moving in from that side. Eyesight, movement and sensation is quite normal on the opposite side. This condition is known as a hemiplegia. Finally, damage to the visual cortex at the back of the brain may cause total blindness resulting from a blow to the back of the head.

The right and left eyes have slightly different fields of vision. Each visual field is split into a right and left side. When light rays reach the retinas they are transposed and inverted. These rays travel down the optic nerves to the optic chiasma, where a crossover takes place. All the information from the left side of each eye travels down the optic tract through the lateral geniculate body and the optic radiation to the right visual cortex and vice versa. Later, the images are combined and interpreted by the brain.

Optometrist

Q I've started having painful headaches. People say this can be caused by defective eyesight. Should I have my eyes tested by an optometrist, or is it a medical problem first and foremost?

A Of all the thousands and thousands of people who go to their doctors each year complaining of headaches, only a tiny minority are found to be suffering from defective eyesight.

It is much more likely that you are having tension headaches, or that you are getting migraines—a particularly severe type of headache with a variety of complex causes.

However, if you notice symptoms such as blurring of objects in the distance, or have difficulty reading, or feel that your eyes are tired and strained at the end of the day, it is worth having your eyes tested. If defective sight is the cause of your headaches, glasses will almost certainly cure them.

Q Is it true that you can ruin your sight by wearing someone else's glasses, even if they do seem to improve your vision?

A Strictly speaking, no; but there is little point in trying to avoid the trouble, or the relatively minor expense of going to an optometrist. If you have defective sight, proper glasses will correct it completely; there is no point in making do. Also, you may well give yourself headaches by using the wrong glasses. Babies and young children, however, can be seriously affected by wearing the wrong glasses.

Q My mother—in her seventies—has more and more difficulty with her sight. Even her new glasses seem to be no help. Why is this?

A Not all problems with the eyesight can be corrected by an optometrist. Cataracts—the clouding of the eye lens—require surgery, not spectacles. Equally, the retina—the light-sensitive area at the back of the eye on which the image forms—can degenerate in old age. This is something neither spectacles nor surgery will help.

Testing eyes and prescribing glasses where necessary is the work of the optometrist—who is not medically qualified but is trained to diagnose eye defects.

There are three basic types of eye problem which call for the services of an optometrist. The first is myopia—short-sightedness—which makes it difficult to see objects in the distance. The second is hypermetropia. Here, objects in the distance are usually well-defined, but there is difficulty reading small print and focusing close up. Finally, there is presbyopia, which we all develop as a natural consequence of ageing. Focusing close-up becomes increasingly difficult,

even if there has been no previous hypermetropia.

Any of these three problems can be complicated by the condition known as astigmatism, in which the eye is unable to focus equally well on vertical and horizontal objects.

If your child wears eyeglasses it doesn't necessarily mean that he cannot take part in the normal rough-and-tumble games: he'll just have to be more careful.

Vision

Eyesight depends on light, and light should be thought of as individual rays travelling in straight lines. These can only change direction if they pass through certain materials—like the glass of a camera lens, or the transparent tissue of the eye. This bending of light rays is called refraction.

By refraction, rays of light are concentrated into the chamber of the eye so that they cast an image on the light-sensitive area at the back known as the retina. The structure of the eye is described in Eyes and eyesight (see pp 479-82).

Most of the refraction takes place at the front of the eye, in the cornea, its transparent 'window'. There is some further refraction as light passes through to the lens at the centre of the eye, but the main

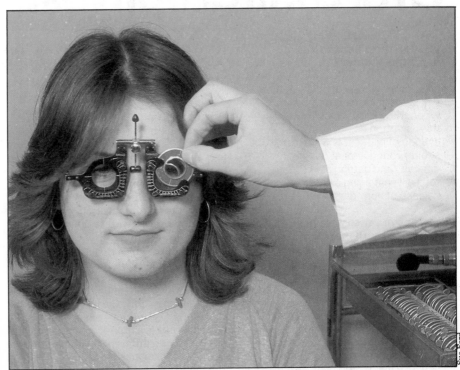

When being fitted for eyeglasses, a special frame is worn into which different lenses are placed to gauge the correct strength.

function of the lens is fine focusing. This is achieved by the circular ciliary, a muscle which surrounds the lens.

The basic reason for poor eyesight—in other words imperfect refractive capacity—is, as might be expected, not a fault in the lens's focusing power, but in the shape of the eyeball itself.

Its ideal shape is more or less spherical, but if it is too long and thin, the cornea tends to be too rounded. The rounder ('stronger') the cornea, the more sharply it bends light rays, with the result that the image is focused in front of the retina, in space, leaving a blur on the retina itself. This is short-sightedness.

Too short an eyeball gives too 'flat' a cornea. It cannot bend the rays sharply enough, and the image falls, in theory, behind the retina. The result is long-sightedness.

In either case, the ciliary muscle tries, but fails, to compensate for the defect.

Astigmatism is caused by an imperfectly curved cornea, and all three conditions are congenital and hereditary.

Visiting the optometrist

Disorders of focusing, then, are what an optometrist looks for.

His basic item of equipment is the test chart, which is usually positioned six metres (or 20 feet) from the patient.

The letter at the top is of a size which can be read at 60 metres (196 feet) by someone with normal sight. The next row down can be read at 36 metres (118 feet), then each succeeding one at 24, 18, 12, 9, 6, 5 metres respectively.

If you can read the seventh row at six metres, your sight is normal. This is called 6/6 vision (or 20/20 vision when measured in feet as it is in the US). The first number refers to your distance from the chart and the second number to the row you can read.

The optometrist will get you to look at the chart while wearing a special frame. By fitting a combination of lenses into this, and asking you how clearly you can read the appropriate row of letters, it can be discovered what strength of lens is required to give you 6/6 vision.

At the same time, the optometrist will peer into your eye with a retinascope, which enables him to observe whether the patient is long- or short-sighted. It also shows when the correct strength or combination of lenses has been put into the frame. Incidentally, this is usually different for each eye.

If the same strength of lens is found with both tests, the optometrist has confirmation of your requirement, and on this basis prescribes spectacles (see pp 2084-6). The retinascope is needed to test astigmatism too, and the glasses ordered for you will be designed, if necessary, to correct this defect.

Finally, your optometrist will advise on whether you can wear contact lenses, instead of ordinary spectacles (see page 316), and when you should return to have your sight re-tested.

Oral contraceptives

Q Can the pill cause loss of interest in sex?

A Some women do find that their interest in sex is decreased when they go on the pill. However, this can often be put right by a change of pill, so it is well worth seeing your doctor about the difficulty and getting a prescription for a pill containing a different balance of hormones.

Q I have varicose veins and I have heard that the pill can make them worse. Is this true?

A If your varicose veins are minor, and you are not in a high risk category for any other reason (medical history, smoking and so forth), you will almost certainly be able to take the pill without extra risks, or greater problems with varicose veins. However, be sure to talk to your doctor about your medical conditions, including the varicose veins, before the pill is prescribed.

Q Should I regularly give the pill a rest to allow my body to get back into the menstrual cycle?

A There is no need to do this frequently, as used to be thought. Neither is there any indication that women who have irregular periods when they are off the pill need to have extra breaks from it. It is generally thought that, provided you are fit and healthy, the pill can be taken without a break for as long as ten years. At that point you might want to consider another form of contraception.

Q Should I tell any doctor I see that I'm on the pill, even if the consultation is about something entirely different?

A Yes, you should. A doctor knows what drugs might interfere with each other, and can avoid prescribing those that will reduce the effectiveness of the pill for you. He or she needs to be aware that you are taking it because this sometimes affects the results of laboratory tests. It is particularly important for a doctor to know what pill a woman is taking if she has to have an operation.

The oral contraceptive – 'the Pill' – is the most reliable reversible method of birth control that exists at present, and one of the most widely used.

Oral contraceptives are made of synthetic hormones similar to those that occur naturally in a woman's body. They prevent pregnancy, and are taken by mouth in pill form. Some oral contraceptives work by stopping ovulation, others by making it difficult for sperm to reach the egg, or for implantation of a fertilized egg in the uterus' wall to take place.

The combination pill is made up of oestrogen and progestogen, and is taken daily for 21 days, followed by seven—or in some cases six—pill-free days in which a withdrawal bleed takes place. The progestogen-only pill (also known as the mini-pill) is taken every day. The triphasic pill is a type of combination pill, but contains a different amount of the two synthetic hormones for different times in the month.

How oral contraceptives work
Different types of pill work in different ways. The combined pill has hormones that are very much like those produced by the body when a pregnancy has occurred. This means that the pituitary gland, which normally sends a message to the ovary to produce its monthly egg acts as if the body is already pregnant; it therefore does not send its egg-stimulating hormone and so no ovulation takes place.

The progestogen-only pill—the mini-pill—does not always stop ovulation from occurring. It makes fertilization by the sperm more difficult by thickening the mucus in the cervical channel leading from the vagina to the uterus (womb), and inhibits the formation of uterine lining which is necessary for the fertilized egg if it is to implant itself. As a result, implantation (and pregnancy) do not take place.

The different types of pill
There are a number of pharmaceutical companies making these pills, and although some of them have different brand names, they are made of identical chemical constituents. Combination pills have two constituents listed; progestogen-only have, of course, just one constituent.

Triphasic pills provide different amounts of the two hormones found in an ordinary pill packet for each week of the cycle, and are said to mimic the menstrual cycle more effectively.

The combination pill is taken for 21

days, with a seven-or six-day break every month. Some women prefer to have a pill every day, so there are some 21-day combination pills that include seven dummy tablets to be taken throughout the fourth week. If you think you will find these pills easier to remember, it is worth asking your doctor for them.

The progestogen-only pills must be taken every day, and can cause changes in periods while they are being taken. Some women don't have any bleeding for several months, others have frequent breakthrough bleeds during the month. Many women have no problems of this sort at all. Bleeding does not mean that the pill isn't working properly, but if you find irregular bleeding troublesome ask your doctor's advice. You are probably not pregnant, but if you are more than two weeks overdue, see your doctor. Which pill you take will be up to you and your doctor. The progestogen-only pill is thought to involve less change of circulatory problems, so is often a first-choice method for those who may be at risk from this kind of disease.

Effect on the body
There are many positive effects of the pill, not least the protection from unwanted pregnancy: 99 per cent or more reliability for the combined pill, 98 per cent for the progestogen-only pill. The pill can also actively protect a woman from certain kinds of disorders, such as the formation of benign breast lumps, can help to clear up acne, and reduce wax in the ears. Since the body is no longer going through the menstrual cycle many of the problems associated with periods—pre-menstrual tension, pain, or heavy bleeding—can be alleviated. Research also suggests that there may be some protection against thyroid and uterine disorders, but this has not yet been confirmed.

Troublesome side-effects may occur at the beginning of a course of pills. Some women find that when they first start taking the pill they feel slightly sick, or that their breasts become a little swollen and sore. Some women who suffer from migraines may find that their condition is made worse by the pill, although for others the opposite is the case. The pill can also affect the ability to wear contact lenses, since the amount of fluid on the surface of the eye may be reduced. It is also thought that the absorption of some

Facts about 'the Pill'

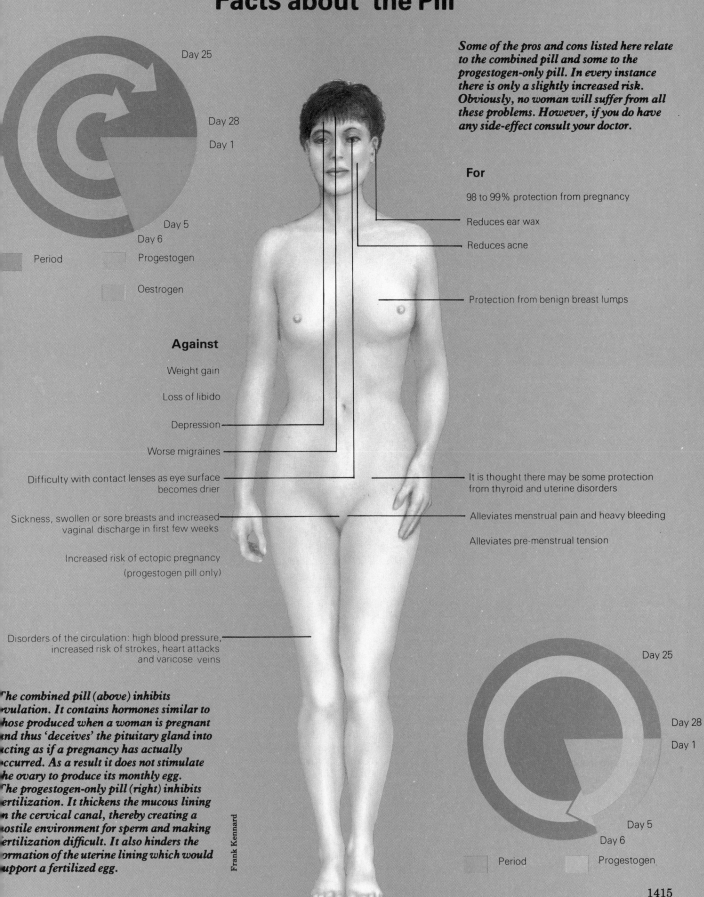

Day 25

Day 28

Day 1

Day 5

Day 6

Period   Progestogen

Oestrogen

Some of the pros and cons listed here relate to the combined pill and some to the progestogen-only pill. In every instance there is only a slightly increased risk. Obviously, no woman will suffer from all these problems. However, if you do have any side-effect consult your doctor.

For

98 to 99% protection from pregnancy

Reduces ear wax

Reduces acne

Protection from benign breast lumps

Against

Weight gain

Loss of libido

Depression

Worse migraines

Difficulty with contact lenses as eye surface becomes drier

Sickness, swollen or sore breasts and increased vaginal discharge in first few weeks

Increased risk of ectopic pregnancy (progestogen pill only)

Disorders of the circulation: high blood pressure, increased risk of strokes, heart attacks and varicose veins

It is thought there may be some protection from thyroid and uterine disorders

Alleviates menstrual pain and heavy bleeding

Alleviates pre-menstrual tension

The combined pill (above) inhibits ovulation. It contains hormones similar to those produced when a woman is pregnant and thus 'deceives' the pituitary gland into acting as if a pregnancy has actually occurred. As a result it does not stimulate the ovary to produce its monthly egg. The progestogen-only pill (right) inhibits fertilization. It thickens the mucous lining in the cervical canal, thereby creating a hostile environment for sperm and making fertilization difficult. It also hinders the formation of the uterine lining which would support a fertilized egg.

Frank Kennard

Day 25

Day 28

Day 1

Day 5

Day 6

Period   Progestogen

Q I've been on the pill for five years, and I now want to become pregnant. When should I go off the pill?

A It is worth going off the pill straight away to give your body time to get back into the menstrual cycle, and you may find that there is a delay before regular periods return. Use other contraceptive methods until you have had two periods, after which time you can try to become pregnant. The delay that sometimes happens between going off the pill and the hoped-for pregnancy may not be due to the pill at all, or it may be that the body needs a little more time before ovulation begins again. If you have tried for a year or more to become pregnant without success, a fertility clinic may be able to help you.

Q I got pregnant when I forgot two pills, but I went on taking them for a time, assuming that I wasn't pregnant. Will this have harmed the baby in any way?

A Taking the pill during the early weeks of pregnancy has not been shown to harm the developing foetus, but research into this is still going on. This is why doctors advise any woman who suspects that she may be pregnant to stop taking the pill and use another method until it has been confirmed whether she is pregnant or not.

Q How often should I have a medical check-up when I'm on the pill?

A You should see your doctor after the first three months on the pill, and thereafter have a check-up every six months. Your blood pressure should be checked, you should have a urine test, and you should be weighed. If your own doctor is not able to do this for you, if you are in Britain it is worth changing to a family planning clinic for advice on contraception, for check-ups—and for the pill itself.

Q Will I gain weight if I go on the pill?

A You may find that you put on a few pounds when you first start taking the pill, and that your weight returns to normal after that.

Taking 'the Pill'

- Taking the combination pill at bedtime, as part of a routine, makes it easier to remember.
- If you do forget one pill, but remember it *within 12 hours*, you will still be protected if you take the rest of the packet at the right time. If you are more than 12 hours late, you will need extra contraceptive precautions for the next 14 days of pill-taking.

- The progestogen-only pill is at its most effective four hours after it is taken, so the best time to do this is at a settled time in early evening.
- If you forget to take the progestogen only pill *for three hours,* you will be unprotected.
- Take the pill first on the first day of your period. Continue to take it *at the same time every day.*

vitamins may be slightly reduced, but this does not need to be a problem: the solution is a healthy diet providing more than enough vitamin intake.

Depression can also be caused by the pill, and in some cases so can loss of libido (sex drive). If you suffer from these symptoms when you are on the pill, discuss them with your doctor, so that an alternative to the combination pill can be considered.

The most dangerous side-effect of the combination pill is the increased likelihood of blood circulatory disorders, such as high blood pressure, thrombosis, heart attacks and strokes. These affect only a tiny minority of women on the pill, and the risk has been greatly reduced by the introduction of those pills containing a lower dose of hormones. However, because the pill does increase the likelihood of these disorders, prospective pill-

users must be carefully screened to see if they are particularly at risk. Your own medical history, and that of your family, will need to be studied. Smoking, being overweight, and being over 35 years of age all increase the risk of these disorders, so women who are in any of these categories are often advised not to use the combination pill. The progestogen-only pill does not seem to carry such risks, and is the one most often prescribed for older women.

The progestogen-only pill is not quite so effective in preventing pregnancy as the combined pill. There is a tiny risk that if an egg is fertilized it will implant itself outside the womb, since the uterine lining is not soft or spongy enough to receive it. This is called an ectopic pregnancy, and it can take place in one of the Fallopian tubes. The risk of it happening is very small indeed, but it is a dangerous condition, needing immediate treatment. Any pain in the lower abdomen should be reported to your doctor.

The return of the menstrual cycle may sometimes be delayed once a woman is off the pill, but it is now thought that it does not affect fertility in the long run.

The choice of which pill is best for you to start off with will be made by your doctor. Most women start with a low-dose combination pill, and are given three months' supply. Any immediate side-effects should be discussed with your doctor on your next visit, or sooner if you feel that they are serious.

Your doctor will advise you to start taking the combination pill on either day one or day five of your next period. If it is the latter, you will need to take additional contraceptive precautions (sheath or diaphragm: see pp 317-21) for 12 days after your first pill-taking day. After that time you are protected by the pill and do not need any extra protection. The combination pill should be taken at whatever time of day is most convenient for you. Many women find that taking it last thing at night becomes part of a routine which is easy to remember. If a pill is forgotten, but you are not more than 12 hours late in remembering to take it, you will still be protected as long as you continue to take the rest of the packet normally. If you are more than 12 hours late you will need to use additional contraceptive precautions for the next 14

Ron Sutherland

days of pill-taking, to make provision for the build-up of hormonal protection.

The progestogen-only pill will be taken first on day one of your period, and must be taken *at the same time every day*, since it is not quite so effective in protecting you against conception as the combination pill. You will need to take additional precautions for the first 14 days. Progestogen-only pills are at their

A woman taking the pill is able to lead a full and satisfying life, free of anxiety about unwanted pregnancy and of many of the discomforts that can accompany periods.

most effective four hours after they are taken, so it is best to do this at a regular time early in the evening. If you are three or more hours late in remembering to take the progestogen-only pill, you should consider yourself unprotected.

The effectiveness of both sorts of pill may be affected by a stomach upset (either vomiting or diarrhoea), as it could mean that the pill has not been absorbed. Other drugs, such as some antibiotics, drugs for epilepsy, sedatives and pain-killers, can also reduce the effect of the pill. Always check with your doctor if you are given any drug, to make sure that there is no risk of this happening.

Coming off the pill
How long a woman stays on the pill will depend on a number of factors, but doctors do recommend that the pill should not be used continuously for more than 10 years, since its very long-term effects are still not fully known.

Women who have to have any major surgery, or who are confined to bed for a time or have a leg in plaster, are advised to come off the pill until they are well again, since these conditions in themselves increase the risk of circulatory problems. Anyone who takes the combination pill would almost certainly have to come off it six weeks before an operation. A woman should, in fact, discuss this point with her doctor, whatever pill she is taking.

Common problems and solutions

Missed one combination pill but have remembered within 12 hours.	Take the missed pill immediately, take the next at its usual time, continue with the rest of the packet as normal.
Missed one combination pill but did *not* remember within 12 hours.	Take the missed pill immediately, the next at its usual time, and the rest of the packet as normal. Protection may have stopped so use additional contraceptive precautions for the next 14 days.
Diarrhoea or vomiting	Continue to take pills as normal, but use additional precautions for the next 14 days.
No period in the pill-free week.	Check with your doctor whether you are pregnant and so whether to start the next packet of pills or not. Until you see him, use a diaphragm or sheath (both with spermicide).
More than three hours late taking a progestogen-only pill.	You are no longer protected. Use another contraceptive for the next 14 days. Keep taking the pills at the regular time, starting with the one you forgot.

Organ removal

Q If I have a lung removed, will the space that it leaves mean that my chest will collapse?

A No. Your remaining lung will soon spread out to fill much of the cavity. In doing so, it will increase in size, which means that its air spaces will grow, too. This in turn means that more oxygen will come into contact with the blood pumping through. In a few months, the single lung will be able to do the work of two, with no loss of efficiency.

Q I just cannot believe that I will look the same again after having my breast removed. Anyway, isn't an artificial breast most uncomfortable?

A Yours is a fair question, and the best answer is simply to have a look at someone who has had a mastectomy, and now wears an artificial breast. You will not be able to tell the difference.
More to the point, an artificial breast—a prosthesis—is not uncomfortable. However, you will be given a special soft one, usually made of foam rubber, to wear until your chest has healed.

Q With one ovary removed, can I still get pregnant?

A Normally, the egg is released from one or the other of your two ovaries on alternate months, so that after one has been removed you may find it takes longer to become pregnant.
Some women ovulate more from one ovary than the other, in which case the chance of conception depends on which ovary is removed.

Q My husband is having his prostate gland removed. Will it affect our sex life?

A The prostate, situated immediately below the bladder is, strictly speaking, one of the male sex organs: it secretes part of the fluid in which the sperm are contained. Lack of such fluid is no hindrance to a fulfilling sex life. Moreover, it does not secrete sex hormones, so the gland's absence, or the removal of part of it, will not affect your husband's performance.

There are few better examples of the human body's astonishing adaptability than its capacity to survive – in good working order – after an organ has been removed.

It is common knowledge, indeed common sense, that a human being can survive with only one eye. Less obvious is the fact that we can do well without one of our two lungs, kidneys, testicles or ovaries.

Moreover, the stomach—which is not duplicated—can be removed entirely, and provided appropriate surgery is performed the patient will be capable of normal digestion in the intestine.

Likewise the larynx, the 'voice box' situated in the throat, can be removed, and the patient learn to talk by means of a specialized burping action.

Some organs, especially the liver, have no 'twin' but instead consist of several 'units', one of which can be removed completely without endangering the whole because of its powers of regeneration.

Why remove an organ?

The obvious, but of course not the only reason for removing an organ is because it has become diseased to the extent that it is a danger to the rest of the body. So, for example, a breast in which a cancerous tumour or lump has developed must be removed, wholly or partially, as early as possible before the cancer spreads.

Accidents—especially car accidents—account for a significant number of organ removals: ruptured spleens or kidneys, causing, at the very least, dangerous internal bleeding, are the all too typical result of being violently thrown against the steering wheel.

What can and cannot be removed

Obviously we can survive the removal of any organ with a pair, provided the other organ is in good condition.

We can also manage without an appendix, the tonsils, the adenoids, gall bladder and spleen. These have no pair, but their function does not need to be maintained because tens of thousands of years of changing living and eating habits have made them partially, or wholly unnecessary to the survival of the individual. In the same way, the womb is essential for reproduction, but not for the individual's survival.

The decision to remove an organ

In spite of the body's ability to adapt, the decision to remove an organ will, of course, never be taken lightly.

One of the chief considerations before deciding to operate will be whether to perform a partial or full removal. Wherever possible, the surgeon opts for removal of only the unhealthy part, and he or she will go to the greatest lengths to preserve even the smallest area of healthy tissue.

The thyroid is an example of an organ which is seldom removed completely. It controls our growth and metabolism, or the body's chemical rate, and for varying reasons can become over-active, with resulting ill-effects on, for example, the

Organ removal often leaves an almost invisible scar, as with this girl's appendicectomy. The surgeon was able to make the incision along a skin crease.

Ron Sutherland

heart. The surgeon's aim is simply to remove enough to put its hormone production back in balance.

The same applies to the ovaries: the surgeon tries to leave behind enough healthy tissue for them to continue to secrete hormones.

Another consideration is how much additional surgery will be required. When removing some organs, considerable 'plumbing' difficulties occur, quite apart from the obvious necessity of joining or tying off blood vessels. Take away someone's stomach, for instance, and it becomes necessary to join the oesophagus (down which food travels towards the stomach) to the intestine.

The heart and liver present more serious dilemmas. A diseased heart can be removed and replaced with a transplant, but the candidate for the operation needs, potentially, to be mentally and physically capable of undertaking the strict regime of medication which will follow. This is a lot to ask of someone who has been living for some time with heart disease.

Obviously a surgeon wants to avoid transplanting if possible: it can be effective, but the risk of rejection is unavoidable. In the case of a diseased liver, a transplant is sometimes possible, but the burning question is how much of the organ has been affected—by a cancer for example—and therefore whether the more satisfactory course of partial removal is possible.

After the operation

Most of the problems associated with organ removal disappear as the body adapts to the loss. People who have a lung removed are breathless at first, but later recover most of their breathing capacity. Minor adjustments to the diet are necessary after stomach removal. Some discomfort under the arm is felt after breast removal, which usually disappears with appropriate exercise.

If a hormone-secreting organ such as an ovary or thyroid is removed in its entirety, it will be necessary to find alternative ways of controlling the hormone level. Usually this means taking hormone by mouth.

Probably the biggest problem is psychological: how to get used to living without an organ. Your doctor should explain that one of the chief marvels of the human body is just this ability to survive loss. Moreover the experience of organ removal can have positive advantages: after removal of the womb, a woman's sex life can actually improve as she is no longer beset with the pain and bleeding of uterine disorders.

And it is surprising how many relationships have actually been improved by the re-thinking of life's purpose, the underlining of mutual needs, and the challenge which goes hand-in-hand with facing an operation of this sort.

Organs which may be removed

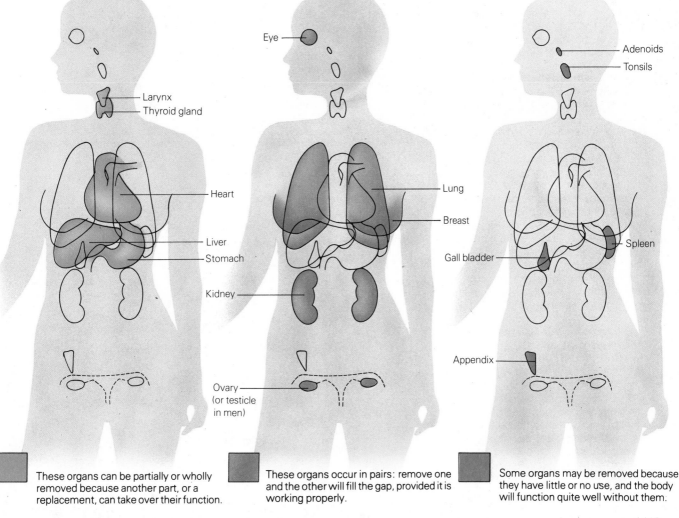

These organs can be partially or wholly removed because another part, or a replacement, can take over their function.

These organs occur in pairs: remove one and the other will fill the gap, provided it is working properly.

Some organs may be removed because they have little or no use, and the body will function quite well without them.

Orgasm

Orgasm – the climax of sexual arousal – has been called the most exquisite of all physical sensations. What happens to the body during orgasm, and how strongly does the mind govern human sexual response?

An orgasm is simply a reflex response to sexual stimulation. But while physical stimulation is essential the mind plays a vital role too.

Lack of sexual attraction or emotional involvement, worries about sex or tension in other areas of life all affect the ability to reach orgasm. Frank and open discussion is therefore necessary to overcome difficulties that may arise (see Intercourse, pp 862-863).

Male orgasmic problems

Most men find that reaching orgasm is relatively easy. Problems can stem from the inability to maintain the plateau phase, the second stage in the orgasmic cycle, when the penis is erect (see Erection and ejaculation, pp 466-467). This can result in either premature ejaculation (when a climax takes place very quickly after arousal has begun) or the loss of erection. Rarely there is a physical reason for this, though in som cases other factors such as drugs fo treating depression or high blood pres sure, or over-indulgence in alcohol, ca make arousal or orgasm difficult. A ma who is experiencing problems shoul consult his doctor to see that all is we physically.

The most common reason for difficulty with orgasm is psychological. A man ma find it easy to maintain an erection an have a satisfying climax by mastur bation, but fail to do so when he is with partner. Some men worry about their per formance and fear failure; others fin that lovemaking makes them feel s nervous and over-excited that the climax before sexual intercourse begins Both of these problems can begin afte one unsatisfactory occasion, leading t anxiety from then on.

Discussion with a partner is helpful s that the man does not feel under so much

The male orgasm

During the male orgasm, the sperm which has mixed with seminal fluid is forced into the urethra by the prostate gland. The muscles around the urethra give a number of rapid involuntary contractions, forcing the semen out of the penis at high pressure. Three of four major bursts of semen are followed by weaker, more irregular contractions.

The female orgasm

The female orgasm begins as a build-up of sensation around the genitals. Before orgasm there is a feeling of tension, when all the small pelvic muscles surrounding the vagina and uterus contract. The orgasm is felt as a series of rhythmical muscular contractions — first around the outer third of the vagina and spreading upward to the uterus.

pressure to perform. Sex therapy also has a high success rate, and often gives the man an opportunity to learn more about his sexuality and to relax about it.

Female orgasmic problems

Women often find it more difficult to have orgasms. In some cases there may be a physical problem such as an unusually over-developed hymen, or an inflammation of the vagina or bladder or a shrinkage of the vaginal lining after menopause, all of which can produce pain on intercourse (dyspareunia). In other cases the libido (sex drive) can be affected by drugs the woman is taking, including the Pill. Women who are experiencing such difficulties should see their doctor.

Many women are able to have orgasms through masturbation on their own, but find it impossible to climax when they are with their partner. This may simply be a question of technique: the woman may need direct clitoral stimulation but her partner may only be willing to have intercourse and nothing else.

Other women find it difficult to ask for what they want, so their partners are unaware that different techniques are needed. The unvarying pattern of cursory foreplay followed by intercourse can also cause difficulties, since what a man may consider to be merely the preliminaries to 'real' sex—that is, intercourse—may be what the woman finds most pleasurable and stimulating. She may be just about to reach climax, but because direct clitoral stimulation ceases, she is unable to do so. To overcome this, either the woman or her partner should continue to stimulate her clitoris manually during intercourse.

Some women have never had an orgasm, either alone or with a partner. The reasons for this are various and include simple lack of knowledge and a fear of insisting that their partner help to satisfy them. Therapists advise women who have never had an orgasm to explore their bodies and find out about their sexual response through masturbation, either manually or by using a vibrator. Once they begin to have orgasms, they can communicate their desires and appropriate techniques to their partners.

Almost every couple can achieve a satisfactory sex life once they have relaxed about it, whether through therapy or just by talking about it.

Ron Sutherland

Orthodontics

Q I am 28 years old and have overlapping front teeth. Am I too old to have them fixed?

A No. Orthodontic treatment can be carried out on adults. It tends to take longer than when it is done in childhood; but provided you can accept the idea of wearing an appliance, it may be possible for your teeth to be corrected. Very severe discrepancies of tooth position are sometimes beyond the scope of orthodontics, even in childhood, and occasionally it may be necessary to give surgical treatment.

Q My daughter's teeth are very crooked and unsightly. Every time I speak to my dentist about this he tells me that he cannot consider giving orthodontic treatment until she improves her oral hygiene. I have great confidence in the dentist and have been his patient for many years, but I feel his attitude is rather unreasonable. What should I do?

A I'm afraid you will just have to nag her until she does clean her teeth properly. Your dentist is quite right in refusing treatment without satisfactory oral hygiene. Unless your daughter cleans her teeth and gums thoroughly she will probably lose her teeth when she is an adult. Also, wearing orthodontic appliances without cleaning the teeth properly can result in gum disease and tooth decay. This is because the presence of an appliance may make an existing oral hygiene problem worse.

Q Is there any danger that wearing an orthodontic appliance might damage my teeth?

A Provided you clean your teeth well to prevent plaque from accumulating, the presence of bands or wires on the teeth will not cause damage. If the appliance becomes a reservoir of bacterial plaque, however, tooth decay will result.

Q Is wearing an orthodontic appliance painful?

A No. There may be a slight discomfort initially, but within a few days this feeling disappears.

Uneven or protruding teeth need not be a cause of lifelong embarrassment. In most cases they can be fully corrected by orthodontic treatment.

Orthodontics is a branch of dentistry. It is concerned with correcting the position of teeth which are irregular and correcting any fault in the way upper and lower teeth come together, or bite. This form of treatment usually requires using appliances, such as braces, which move the teeth into their correct position. In cases where the teeth are too crowded together, some of them may have to be extracted to provide the necessary space for them to grow normally.

The normal position of teeth

Ideally, the upper and lower rows of teeth – the dental arches – should be symmetrical, with teeth in even positions. There should be no sign of overlapping (crowding) or spaces. The upper arch should be slightly larger than the lower one so that when the teeth bite, the upper teeth all fit just outside the lower ones.

This perfect arrangement of teeth is found only rarely. Just as people vary in

Normal bite

Normal bite: the upper and lower rows of teeth should be symmetrical, with teeth being in even positions, not overlapping or overcrowded. The upper teeth should fit just around the lower teeth, the upper arch being slightly larger than the lower. Such an ideal rarely exists. Incorrect bite: malocclusion occurs when the front teeth grossly overlap or protrude over the bottom row. Teeth may be spaced or overcrowded. Treatment for malocclusion is by a fixed appliance.

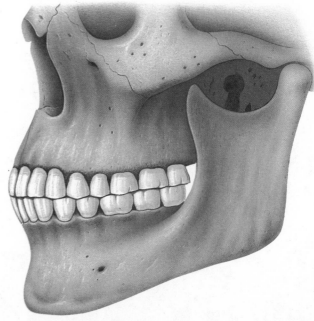

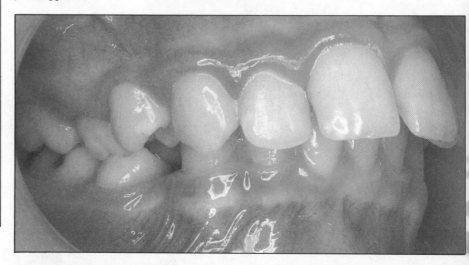

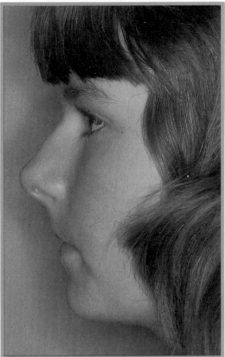

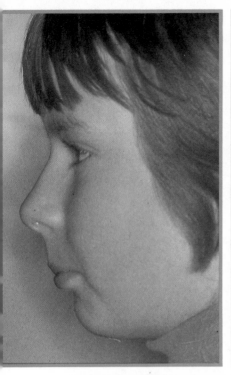

their height and in other physical characteristics, so they vary in the position of their teeth and structure of their jaws. Slight variations from the ideal pattern do not affect the health of the teeth or a person's appearance. In fact, many people would consider a minor degree of tooth irregularity attractive.

Orthodontic treatment is required when teeth are so uneven that they spoil the individual's appearance, or cause dental problems, or when they do not give a proper bite. The latter condition is known as malocclusion.

Causes of irregularities

Most of the factors that determine the size and position of the teeth, as well as the size of the jaw, are inherited. The characteristics inherited from both parents will therefore affect how the teeth will grow. For example, a child who has a father with large teeth and a mother with small jaws may have a combination of teeth and jaws which do not match, and may have overcrowded teeth.

In some cases, environmental factors will influence how teeth develop. Persistent finger- or thumb-sucking, for example, will change the position of the incisors (the four central teeth in both the upper and lower jaws). Tooth position may also be affected by diseases of the jaw, but this only occurs in a very small minority of cases.

Where significant irregularity is present, several problems may occur.

Teeth which are overlapping are more difficult to clean and this may result in gum disease and tooth decay. An incorrect bite, where the lower incisor teeth bite against the roof of the mouth instead of against the upper teeth, may give rise to inflammation of a part of the palate.

In some cases, when the teeth come together they bite on the wrong side of the teeth in the opposite jaw. This may have damaging effects on the jaw joints because the patient needs to bite to one side to avoid teeth which are in the way.

Incorrect bite: malocclusion

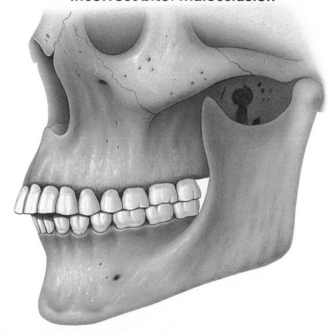

The photographs above show a child before and after orthodontic treatment. Note the striking changes in her profile. The photographs below show the same child's teeth in their original state and during and after treatment. The teeth were irregular, spaced, protruding and malloccluded. A fixed orthodontic appliance was used to correct these irregularities and was worn for three years. After that time, her bite became regular, with the teeth in correct position.

Mike Courtney

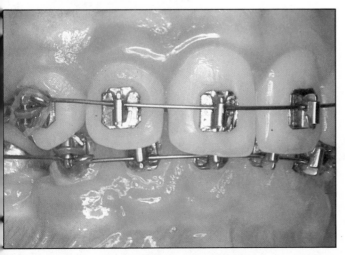

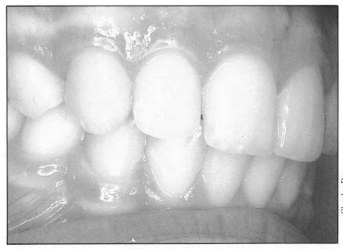

Charles Day

Grossly irregular or spaced teeth may cause problems with speech, although this is unusual. However, a person may feel embarrassment because of irregular teeth and treatment to correct the irregularity is frequently requested precisely for this reason.

Treatment

The time when treatment is given depends largely on the rate of development of the teeth. It is sometimes possible to start before all the milk teeth have fallen out but it is often necessary to wait for the premolars (the teeth in front of the molars) and permanent canine teeth (those next to the incisors) to come through – usually between 11 and 12.

When there appears to be a need for treatment, this is discussed with the patient and in the case of a child, with his parents. Impressions of teeth are taken from which plaster models are made. X-rays are taken to confirm the presence of and to locate any teeth which have not yet grown, and to assess the jaw's shape. The patient's face and teeth may be photographed. A treatment is then worked out.

Why extractions are necessary

Crowding of teeth usually occurs when the tooth size is so large that there is no enough space for all the teeth. Patient who have only a mild degree of over crowding are often best advised to accep the situation. However, where it is mor severe, treatment is indicated to hel avoid the development of other problems such as difficulty in cleaning the teeth adequately.

At one time it was thought that over crowded teeth could be aligned simply b enlarging the dental arches. Althoug this treatment helps in the short term i has been shown that overcrowding wil eventually recur. In most cases, the onl long-term treatment is to extract some c the teeth already in place. This provide sufficient space for the rest of the teeth t come in and develop normally.

Careful consideration is given t choosing which teeth to extract. When al the teeth are in good condition, the firs premolars are frequently removed. How ever, if certain teeth are very heavil filled or are badly positioned, these teeth

Children who persist in thumb-sucking onc their permanent teeth come through may require orthodontic treatment (below).

Ron Sutherland

Removable orthodontic appliances

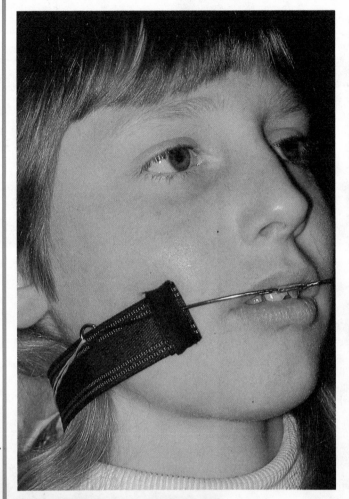

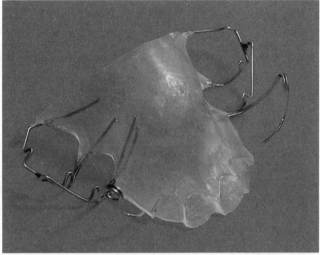

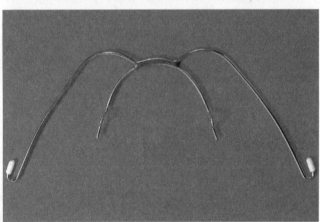

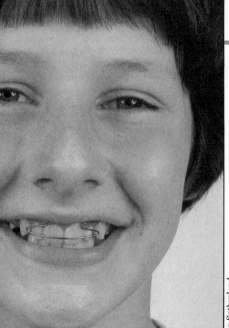

There are various types of removable orthodontic appliance, one of which is illustrated (top right). An extra-oral traction appliance (above) can be fitted in some cases. The two appliances are worn by the patient at night (above left).

will be extracted instead of the first premolars.

After the extractions have been carried out there is often a spontaneous improvement in the positions of adjacent teeth which tend to move into the space. However, such improvement is usually insufficient to correct the irregularity of the teeth fully, and an appliance will also be required.

Orthodontic appliances

There are two main types of orthodontic appliances: functional and mechanical. Both types move the teeth into the correct position and hold them there until they will maintain their place unaided. Functional appliances improve the way in which the upper and lower teeth meet, or bite. They move the entire dental arch as one unit, unlike fixed and removable appliances which move individual teeth. They are therefore only effective when a child is growing rapidly. For example, if all the upper teeth are too far forward, a functional appliance at the right age can mould the upper arch back as it grows, insuring a better contact with the lower arch when biting.

Mechanical appliances do not necessarily require growth in order to work, although their effect is more rapid during a phase of growing. The two main types of mechanical appliance are removable ones (which the patient can take out) and fixed appliances (those that are bonded to the teeth). Fixed appliances exert a greater degree of control on the teeth and produce movement in any direction. Removable appliances can only produce a tilting action on the teeth.

In general, fixed appliances are used in

Q What special precautions are required while wearing an orthodontic appliance?

A The most essential one is to maintain good oral hygiene. Removable appliances should be taken out at least twice a day, and teeth thoroughly cleaned with a brush and with dental floss. The appliance should also be scrubbed using a tooth-brush and tooth-paste. This should keep it free from any bacteria that may have accumulated.

Fixed appliances are more difficult to clean and therefore take longer to attend to. The use of a very small tooth-brush is the most effective way of cleaning around them. If the gum begins to bleed on contact with a tooth-brush, this suggests that some inflammation of the gums is present and even more thorough brushing is required. This may make the gum bleed at the time, but if thorough brushing is maintained, before long the gum will become firmer and then will no longer bleed on brushing.

If any problems with your gums occur, see your dentist.

Q I have heard that badly misplaced teeth can be transplanted. Is this true?

A It is possible to transplant completely buried teeth, but there must be adequate space for them. This method of treatment is used mainly in cases where upper canine teeth have failed to erupt. This occurs in about 2 per cent of people, and the teeth concerned remain below the surface—usually in the palate. Such a tooth can be removed surgically and then immediately inserted into a specially prepared socket in the right place.

After the transplant has been done it is necessary to hold the tooth in place with a splint while healing takes place (usually for three weeks). While most teeth that have been transplanted remain in good condition, a small number have to be removed subsequently either because of infection or because the root has been destroyed.

This technique is useful when teeth cannot be moved into the correct position by any other means, but it does not provide a substitute for routine orthodontic methods in cases where many teeth are incorrectly placed.

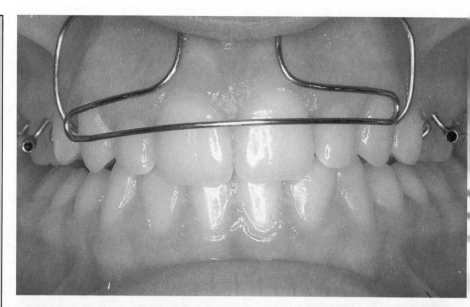

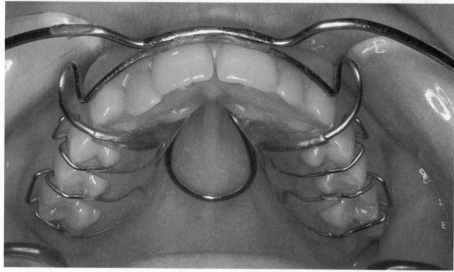

the more complex cases, where rotation or bodily movement of teeth is required. Removable appliances are utilized in cases where the teeth can simply be tilted back to their correct position.

Generally, removable appliances need to be worn day and night if they are to move the teeth effectively. The appliance is adjusted by the dentist, but there may be 'auxiliary' components such as elastic bands which the patient must change.

Extra oral traction (the application of force to the teeth from a source outside the mouth) is sometimes applied either to removable or fixed appliances. In these cases, additional force needs to be applied to move teeth back further.

Orthodontic appliances usually need adjustment at monthly intervals, and treatment generally takes between 18 months and two years. Although there is often some initial discomfort, after a few days the patient is usually perfectly comfortable wearing the appliance.

This shows the front view of a removable orthodontic appliance in place (top), and a view of the mouth when extra-oral traction is fixed permanently to it (bottom). The whole appliance is worn 14 hours a day.

Outlook

Treatment of malocclusion is possible because the bone which supports the teeth respond and adapts to light pressure and so teeth can be pushed into place. Irregular teeth can be made even and to a considerable extent the bite of the teeth can be corrected. It is doubtful however if the shape of the jaws themselves can be improved by orthodontic appliances, but nevertheless correction of tooth position can result in a great improvement in the facial profile.

Patients with very severe discrepancies of the jaw position generally require surgical treatment, although this is often facilitated by preliminary orthodontic realignment of the teeth.

Orthopaedics

Q My son has been put into a whole body plaster after an accident. As he won't be able to wash for a while, won't his skin suffer?

A The skin manages perfectly well covered up by plaster. It continues to grow and sheds masses of scales so that when the plaster comes off the limb looks rather dirty and the skin has the texture of sandpaper. All of this gets better within a few weeks.

Q Is it a better idea to have a bone set with plaster or a pin, or is the choice not so straightforward?

A It is always better to let nature do it herself. A pin, or plate or other piece of metal is only used if the orthopaedic surgeon does not think that he can get the fracture to unite firmly without doing so. The choice of whether a pin or a bone graft is used is entirely up to the surgeon and depends upon the type of injury sustained, so the choice is not simple.

Q I am due to have a replacement knee joint. Will this offer the same strength and range of movements?

A Clearly, a mechanical replacement cannot compete with the perfection of a normal knee joint. There will be some limitation of movement, particularly in the twisting action that knees are able to perform and that the hinge of the replacement joint will not. However, you need have no worry about its strength.

Q After I had my broken leg mended I found that it was a little shorter than the other one. Can an orthopaedic surgeon or practitioner do anything about this?

A No. Your leg is shorter because you presumably suffered a severe fracture and lost a few bone fragments as a result. This bone cannot be replaced and so your leg cannot be lengthened.

Orthopaedics is the surgical speciality which treats diseases and injuries to bones and soft tissues. Orthopaedic surgeons deal with a wide range of problems – from sprains to replacing entire joints.

A broken bone left to its own devices will usually heal, or in medical terminology, unite. The orthopaedic surgeon tries to make sure that the fracture unites in a good position so that the limb will function well afterwards. He also makes certain that no complications develop while the fracture is healing.

Treatment of fractures

A limb fracture (breakage) is usually diagnosed in the casualty department or emergency room of a hospital. An uncomplicated fracture will be set there and then, often under an anaesthetic, and a plaster may be applied to hold the set in place. The patient will not generally see the orthopaedic consultant until he visits the out-patient department to have the plaster inspected and X-rays taken – to ensure that the bone ends are fitting firmly together and that the splint is holding up to everyday wear and tear.

The consultant will decide if a new plaster needs to be applied and when the old plaster is ready to come off. Most simple fractures of the arm need to stay in plaster for between four to six weeks. A leg fracture, however, takes twice as long because the limb is weight-bearing.

Plaster is the most commonly used method of treating fractures. It has its limitations, though: some areas of the body, such as the shoulder and hip, are difficult to hold in plaster; in addition, plaster covers the skin, which may itself have suffered severe injury and need careful watching. It also stops joints moving and they may become stiff.

Having a plaster cast removed from a leg is a messy and sometimes ticklish business – if this girl's face is anything to go by. But it's seldom painful.

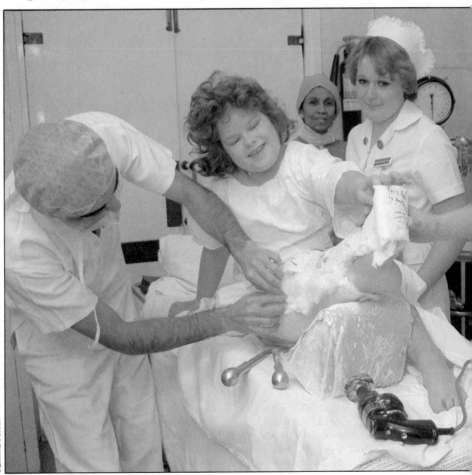

Camilla Jessel

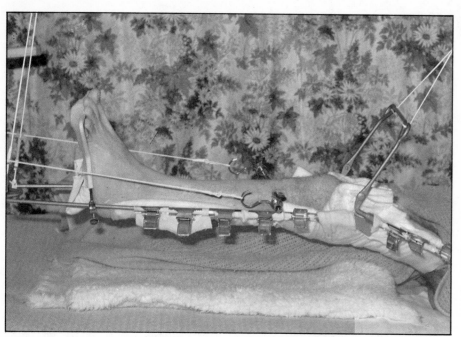

Reduction and internal fixation

The orthopaedic surgeon may decide that a fracture needs to be operated upon. This may be necessary when it is clear that the bones cannot be brought into a satisfactory position by other means, or when the fracture would confine the patient to bed for a long time.

In this sort of operation an incision is made in the skin along the length of the bone which is then exposed by pulling back the muscles surrounding it. The periosteum—a layer of tissue which coats the bone—is peeled back from the fracture, and the ends of the bones are carefully cleaned and fitted together, or 'reduced'. The ends are joined together with a piece of metal: this is called internal fixation. Usually a strip of metal is screwed along the length of the bone.

A fractured leg in traction. The purpose of traction is to pull the bone ends apart and align them properly.

Putting the leg in traction

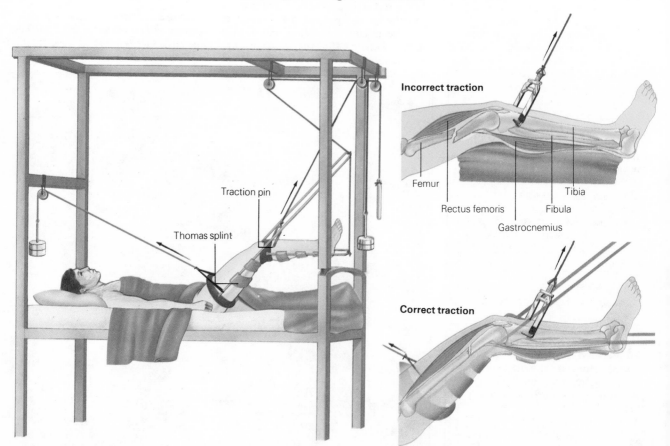

Traction pin

Thomas splint

Incorrect traction

Femur

Rectus femoris

Gastrocnemius

Tibia

Fibula

Correct traction

Aziz Khan

Here the shaft of the femur has been fractured. Traction must be applied parallel to the fracture in order to make sure that the alignment of the fractured bone ends is perfect (above). The calculations are complicated, since many different forces have to be counterbalanced in order to achieve the right alignment. Not least of these forces is the pressure exerted by the leg muscles. The leg must be held in exactly the right position to counteract and compensate for the pull of the muscles – the position is wrong (top), correct (above), since all the relevant forces have been considered and the right alignment achieved.

crossing the fracture site: a procedure known as 'plating'. On some occasions a long nail is used to hold the bone ends in position and this is driven up through the hollow shaft of the bone through its entire length.

Pin and plate operation

When fixing the head of the thigh bone a pin is driven in from the side of the femur and up the centre of the broken neck, ensuring that the pin stops just short of the joint. This is then held in place with a metal plate screwed to the side of the femur. This procedure is known as a 'pin and plate' operation. The great advantage of fixation by pinning or screwing is that the patient can be up and about within days of the operation and a plaster cast is usually unnecessary. The pin and plate operation is particularly suitable for elderly people who fall and fracture their hips. The metal used is inert and can stay in the body for life without causing any trouble or discomfort to elderly patients.

Traction for fractures

Traction is used almost exclusively for fractures of the leg. After such an injury the muscles tighten up and pull the bone ends past each other, so that the lower fragment rides up to lie alongside the upper fragment. Unless the bone ends are pulled apart and correctly aligned this will result in union of the fracture with some shortening of the limb.

Traction is applied to the lower bone fragment by means of a weight hung from a steel pin driven through the shin bone or heel. The weights are usually suspended from an arrangement of pulleys placed at the end of the bed. Obviously the 200-lb man needs heavier weights than the six-year-old child, and to prevent the weights pulling the patient out of bed the foot end is sometimes placed on blocks. The advantage of traction is that the joints are free to move, and any skin wounds can be watched.

Bone grafting

Some fractures, particularly those of the tibia, fail to unite. In such cases pieces of bone may be taken from another part of the patient's own skeleton and 'grafted'. A favourite site for the donor bone is the pelvis, high up on the hip. Here a strip of bone up to 10 cm (4 in) long can be cut away without any damage or interference to the skeleton. The un-united fracture is cleaned thoroughly and small pieces of bone graft are placed in the fracture. This causes the body to form strong new bone around the bone graft, and sound union of the fracture takes place over a few weeks.

Compound fractures

A compound fracture – where broken bone ends have penetrated the overlying skin – carries a high risk of infection and must be treated carefully. This involves cleaning the wound thoroughly by means of an operation. All the dead muscle and skin is cut away, removing the possibility of infection with bacteria that can cause gangrene. After the wound is cleaned the bone ends can be brought together and

This is an X-ray of a femur fracture repaired by 'pin and plate'. The metal will cause no discomfort to the patient at all.

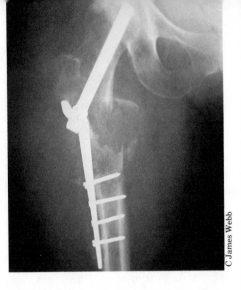

C James Webb

The 'pin and plate'

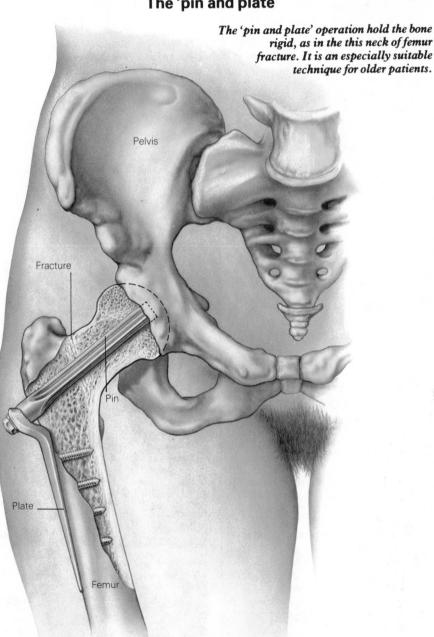

The 'pin and plate' operation hold the bone rigid, as in the this neck of femur fracture. It is an especially suitable technique for older patients.

Pelvis

Fracture

Pin

Plate

Femur

Frank Kennard

Q My little girl has to use braces on her legs to help her walk—she has spina bifida. Will she ever be able to do without these unsightly gadgets?

A The condition known as spina bifida sometimes affects the nerves going to the muscles of the legs, resulting in partial paralysis. There is nothing wrong with the bone. Presumably the reason why your little girl wears braces is that she has partially paralyzed legs. As she grows older, rather more sophisticated gadgets can be used which are far less unsightly.

Q I often hear of soccer players having their knee cartilages removed. Why?

A The knee is unique amongst joints of the body in that it has two triangular wedges of cartilage lying actually within the joint cavity. These act as shock absorbers and take the wear and tear of twisting and running. They are attached quite firmly to the capsule of the joint around the edges and to the bone of the knee joint at the centre. Unnatural twisting movements—such as happen in sport—separate these two points and are liable to tear the cartilage. Once this has happened, the cartilage is permanently damaged and never heals because it has no blood supply. Since it then gets in the way of normal joint movement it must be removed. Surprisingly, it doesn't seem to make too much difference to the use of the knee joint afterwards, as many soccer players are fortunately able to attest.

Q Is it possible to transplant bone from one patient to another?

A In theory, it would be feasible to transplant bone, and in fact bone marrow has been successfully transplanted. However, there are two reasons why bone transplant is not necessary. The first is that there is an abundant supply of bony material in other parts of the patient's own skeleton, and secondly, artificial bone has now been made from a basis of synthetic material which when inserted in the body is invaded by bone-making cells and adopted by the body, as it were.

the skin can then be sewn back into place.

Internal fixation is usually avoided as this makes the possibility of serious infection more likely. If the skin wound cannot be closed with stitches, skin grafting may be necessary.

Ruptured tendon
A rupture of the Achilles tendon (at the back of the heel) is a common injury. The patient experiences sudden pain at the time of the injury and suffers considerable discomfort afterwards. This may be treated by stitching the tendon together, or by putting the ankle in plaster. Tendons take six weeks to join together and during this time they may come apart again or become stuck to the surrounding

The strenuous demands which the sudden moves of soccer makes on the knees means that players are particularly prone to such injuries as torn cartilage (inset).

tissue. This is particularly unfortunate when the tendons leading to the fingers are involved, and very delicate and complicated surgery may be necessary to try to restore movement.

Joint dislocation
Reduction of dislocation is usually a simple matter when the patient is fully relaxed under anaesthetic. However, problems arise when repeated dislocation occurs—for example, after a shoulder injury where the original dislocation has weakened the surrounding tissue. Here surgical reconstruction of the joint capsule is required. Joint injuries often cause stiffening, and physiotherapy may be necessary to improve movement and the strength of muscles after these injuries.

Diseases of the locomotor system
Orthopaedic surgeons treat a variety of conditions not caused by injury. These

include birth defects and deformities in children, arthritic conditions, bone cancers and disorders of the spine. He also treats congenital defects, like congenital dislocation of the hip, a condition which may run in families. The baby is born with the ball of the hip joint fitting poorly in its socket, or not lying in the socket at all. This is usually detected in the first few weeks of life, and when it is, the baby is put in a splint or plaster to hold the legs apart, so that the hip fits firmly in its socket. The hip usually develops normally if treatment is started early enough, but if the baby is more than a few months old, operations may be necessary.

Joint replacement surgery

In recent years advances in engineering and the development of new materials have made it possible to replace entire joints. The commonest such operation is

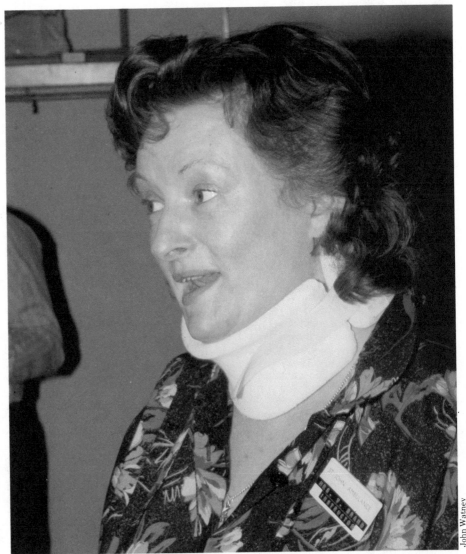

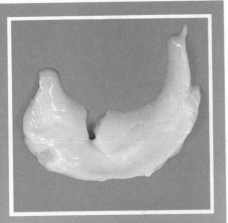

hip joint replacement, where a metal ball and plastic socket are cemented into the thigh bone and hip socket with acrylic cement. This operation is very successful in relieving the pain and stiffness of wear and tear arthritis. Since it is not yet certain how long the artificial hip joint will go on working before it wears out or loosens, surgeons are cautious of doing this operation on people under sixty.

The knee, elbow, shoulder and knuckle joint can be replaced in a similar manner, but these operations are reserved for people suffering from severe inflammatory or rheumatoid arthritis, a disease with a predilection for the small joints that are not necessarily weight-bearing.

Recent advances

Many orthopaedic surgeons now use an instrument called an arthroscope for looking inside the knee joint. The instrument is like a small telescope which the surgeon can insert into the joint through a small puncture wound. He can

A cervical collar provides positive support for the back of the neck and the lower part of the head – support that may be necessary, for example, in cases of whiplash or a similar injury.

then see the condition of the joint and the cartilages, and he can even perform some operations without opening the joint. Advances in this field are improving results in the surgical treatment of many knee injuries.

Some orthopaedic surgeons now perform 'microsurgery': joining together cut nerves and blood vessels that may be no bigger than a matchstick with many fine stitches. This is performed under a large microscope with very delicate instruments, and is the basis for recently publicized operations to reattach severed limbs. In addition, there have been startling new developments in the design of prostheses – artificial replacements for lost limbs – which give new hope for a better life to amputees.

1431

Osmosis

Q I have heard that kidney machines work by osmosis. Is this true?

A It is certainly true that osmosis is a very important factor in the way that kidney machines work. What happens is that the blood of a patient on the machine is allowed to pass along a membrane which has special fluid on its other side, known as dialysis fluid. Waste products pass along the membrane, and the amount of water allowed to pass across depends upon the strength of the dialysis fluid, since osmotic pressure would tend to suck water out of the blood if a strong solution were used, whereas the blood would take up water from a weak one. In emergency situations in hospitals where kidney machines are not available, doctors can achieve exactly the same effect by running fluid in and out of the abdomen.

Q Can osmosis ever stop working in the body?

A No, osmosis is a basic law of nature and as such it will never stop working in the body. However, it doesn't always work to the body's advantage. The osmotic forces of the blood keep the lungs free from fluid under normal circumstances, but if the air sacs (alveoli) should start to fill up with fluid, as they do in cases of infection and heart failure, it can be very difficult to dry the lungs out again: the fluid in them may contain quite a lot of protein and other substances which themselves exert an osmotic force and so tend to suck yet more fluid into the lungs.

Q Does food get from our intestines into the blood by osmosis?

A The main substance carried across the intestinal wall by osmosis is water, which is one of the most important things that the intestine has to absorb. Most of the other important nutrients, such as, proteins, sugar and fats are broken into their basic molecules by the process of digestion and then carried across the intestinal wall by energy-consuming transport mechanisms.

Osmosis is the way in which substances can pass across membranes. It is one of the basic processes that determine how all living things work.

Osmosis is the name given to the process by which water and other solvents can pass across membranes. In the human body every single cell is surrounded by a membrane that keeps the cell's internal contents separate from what is outside it. In fact most of the energy we use up in daily life is not expended on doing things such as walking, or forms of work, but at a cellular level in simply transferring substances to keep the balance in the body exactly correct.

Molecules and osmosis

The membranes that enclose the cells of the body are called semi-permeable membranes. This means that they are made up in such a way that some substances – water, for example – can pass freely from one side to the other, while others, such as a big protein molecule, cannot pass across. As a general rule, the ability of a substance to pass across a semi-permeable membrane is governed by the size of the molecules making it up.

The body contains many different chemical substances, in the form of separate molecules made up of atoms. In some substances the molecules may each

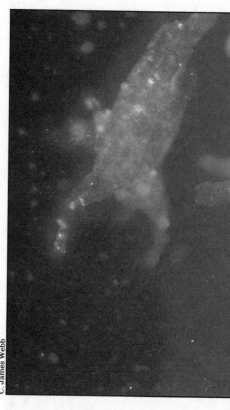

C. James Webb

The process of osmosis

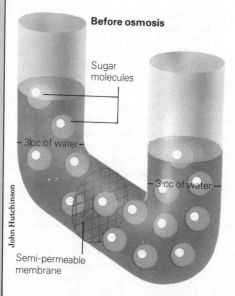

John Hutchinson

Before osmosis

Sugar molecules

– 3cc of water –

– 3cc of water –

Semi-permeable membrane

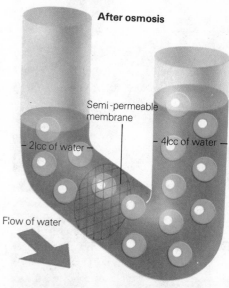

After osmosis

Semi-permeable membrane

– 2cc of water –

– 4cc of water –

Flow of water

If two sugar solutions – one double the strength of the other – are separated by a semi-permeable membrane, osmosis will

occur. Water passes through the barrier from the weaker solution to the stronger until both are the same strength.

The amoeba is a single-cell organism that lives in water and relies on osmosis to keep the right balance between its body fluid and its environment.

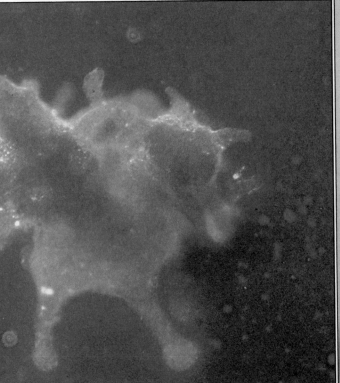

Originally, the tube inside the beaker held a stronger solution. By osmosis the weaker moved across the membrane, and the fluid level in the tube was raised as a result.

be very small like water which contains only three atoms. In others they are very large, containing thousands of atoms.

In general it is water that can pass freely to and fro across a semi-permeable membrane, such as a cell wall. Other molecules, even relatively small ones such as sugar, require special, energy-using transport mechanisms to allow them to pass in and out of cells.

Osmotic pressure

The basis of osmosis is that water will tend to pass from a weaker solution to a stronger one if there is a semi-permeable membrane between them. This can be demonstrated by a simple experiment in which a weak sugar solution is separated from a strong one by such a membrane. The water will tend to pass from the weaker one to the stronger one, making the solutions the same strength. If the experiment is repeated with pure water on one side, the water will start to be sucked into the strong sugar solution by osmosis. Eventually, the level of fluid on the sugar side of the barrier will rise as more and more water crosses, and at a certain point there will

be so much more water on one side than the other that the pressure it exerts will stop any more crossing the barrier. If the level of water containing sugar has risen to 3 cm (1½ in), for example, the original solution is said to exert an osmotic pressure of 3 cm.

Osmosis in the human body

The tendency for water to move from weak to strong solutions is one that has to be controlled very carefully by the body, and so the strength of the solution both inside and outside the cells has to remain more or less constant.

One of the interesting things about osmosis is that the osmotic pressure of a fluid – the amount of water that it would tend to suck into it through a membrane – depends on the number of molecules dissolved in it. For example, a solution containing one million sugar molecules in one litre would have the same osmotic pressure as one with a million different sorts of protein molecules, even though such molecules are hundreds of times larger than a sugar molecule.

Osmosis is important in keeping the blood fluid and therefore able to circulate.

When someone is standing upright, the veins are supporting a long column of blood going right up to the top of the body. This head of pressure might be expected to squeeze all the water in the blood out into the tissues, causing swelling, since the walls of the capillaries at least are freely permeable to water. However, the blood also contains a considerable number of large molecules, such as protein molecules, and these cannot pass out through the walls of the blood vessels. Instead, they exert osmotic 'suction' which keeps the water in the bloodstream and constantly balances the amount of water both inside and outside the walls of the blood vessels.

A striking example of the importance of osmosis is in the various conditions where the level of protein in the blood—starts to fall so that it provides less of an osmotic force. Protein loss occurs in kidney disease, especially in the nephrotic syndrome (see Nephritis, pp 1301-4) and in liver disease. Both these conditions may result in much swelling of the ankles and legs, and even in an accumulation of fluid in the abdomen for the same reasons.

Osteoarthritis

Q I have suffered from osteoarthritis for many years. Can my daughter inherit it?

A Osteoarthritis is not an inherited disease. However there is a tendency for people in the same family to develop osteoarthritis of the hands. This may reflect the fact that members of the same family often have the same sort of interests, and so subject their hands to the same sort of stresses, therefore increasing the likelihood of the disease.

Q I've read that professional footballers often suffer from osteoarthritis. This is worrying because I thought that exercise was good for you. Which is correct?

A Doctors are divided in their opinion about whether sportsmen like footballers really do have a higher rate of the disease. It may be that sportsmen, being active, are more likely to try and get help for minor degrees of osteoarthritis and so come to doctors' notice.

However the general view is that there is a small increase in the disease among professional sportsmen, particularly those who play contact sports like football. Indeed particular sports give rise to particular complaints: professional cyclists get knee problems, while professional footballers get a very unusual form of arthritis in the middle bones of the foot. This is probably due to the fact that these parts suffer from repeated small injuries.

Therefore, to put your mind at rest, we can say that exercise itself is not bad for you, but repeated injuries are, and may be a cause of osteoarthritis.

Q Is it true that damp weather makes osteoarthritis worse?

A This is such a common thing for patients to report that it seems almost bound to be true However there is no obvious explanation of why it should occur. In fact there is nothing to suggest that a cold damp climate makes the disease progress or become more severe. It just seems that people are more aware of the pain that osteoarthritis causes when the weather is cold.

Many people regard aching and painful joints as an inevitable part of ageing. In fact the cause may be a disease called osteoarthritis. Drugs can relieve pain, and in severe cases surgery can effect dramatic improvement.

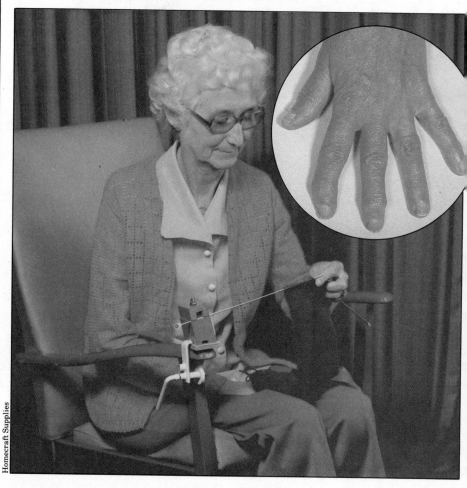

Homecraft Supplies

People whose osteoarthritic fingers have become deformed and stiff (inset) can keep up their hobbies by using ingenious aids.

Osteoarthritis is one of the commonest forms of arthritis. In fact half the population over the age of 50 have some signs of the disease, which can also affect some people in their thirties and forties. Although it is possible to get osteoarthritis, or OA, in almost any joint in the body, there are some joints where it is particularly likely to occur. These include the hips, the knees, the hands, the back and the neck.

Osteoarthritis is painful, and in some cases can be crippling since it reduces the amount of movement in severely affected joints. Treatment is with aspirin or other painkillers, but in severe cases surgery can be performed to replace some of the affected joints.

Causes

Although a great deal is known about how osteoarthritis develops once it actually occurs, the causes of the disease are obscure.

Joints between bones are lined with a membrane called the synovial membrane. This forms a kind of bag surrounding the joint which is filled with synovial fluid. The actual parts of the joint where the bones are in contact with each other are lined with cartilage, and it is the two cartilage surfaces coming into contact with each other that bear the load of the joint. Cartilage itself is made up of a hard network of fibres that contain cartilage producing cells and fluid, so that it provides an excellent lubricated surface for the moving parts of the joint. Osteoarthritis is a disease which results from the alteration in the structure of this cartilage (see Joints, pp 902-5).

In the first stage of osteoarthritis, a number of small clefts appear on the surface of the cartilage and there is an increase in the number of cartilage-producing cells. At this stage the patient may not notice any symptoms or only experience some very slight degree of pain and stiffness.

In the next stage, the cartilage caps to the bone ends begin to wear thin until finally there is no cartilage left and the bone ends bear directly onto one another. There may be considerable destruction of the bone as it is worn away by movements of the joint, and also a thickening of the capsule of the synovial membrane that surrounds the joints.

Unlike cartilage, though, bone is able to repair itself as it gets eaten away, but in osteoarthritis the way in which bone does this around an osteoarthritic joint is disorganized. This can sometimes lead to rough deposits, which do more harm than good to the joint.

It would appear that the cause of osteoarthritis is the continual stress on the joint – hence the name 'wear and tear' arthritis. But this theory does not explain the fact that joints which bear the same amount of weight are not equally affected: that is, the hip and knee are likely to be involved, whereas the ankle is not.

Some factors, however, may predispose a patient to osteoarthritis. For instance a background of repeated small injuries may be a causative factor: sportsmen –

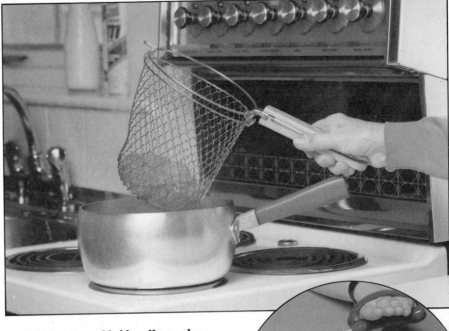

Homecraft Supplies

The thick and moulded handles on these cooking utensils enable osteoarthritis sufferers to deal with food more easily.

footballers for example – are said to get more osteoarthritis than normal, particularly in the feet.

Deformity of the limb or a joint may be another contributing factor, and this may lead to stresses on the joint that are so severe that they amount to repeated injury.

Another factor which makes osteoarthritis more likely is when the nerve supply to a particular joint is interrupted

Treating osteoarthritis

Site	Symptoms	Treatment
Hands	Usually affects the joints between the bones of the fingers, producing characteristic lumps on either side of the furthest joint (Heberden's nodes). The thumb is often involved. Joints are painful on movement	Aspirin and related drugs. Occasionally immobilizing the thumb in plaster may be helpful
Feet	Pain on walking, most commonly in the joint at the base of the big toe	Aspirin and related drugs. Occasionally surgical shoes, or surgery
Ankles	Very rare, unless there is some bone deformity	
Knees	Affects more women than men. Sometimes very little pain. Knock knees can result	Basic treatment is with drugs, but very painful or deformed joints can be treated surgically
Hips	Pain particularly on walking. Can lead to a limp or a 'waddle' if both hips are involved	Initial treatment is aspirin or a related drug. A walking stick may be helpful. Surgery, particularly joint replacement, in more severe cases
Spine	Commonest in the neck. Causes pain and limitation of movement. Neck involvement can lead to blackouts or weakness in arms and legs	Aspirin and other pain-relieving drugs. A neck collar worn at night may be helpful
Shoulder	Rare, unless there has been some injury. Immobility and stiffness are usually more of a problem than pain	Exercises combined with painkilling drugs may help to ease shoulder movement
Elbow	Rare. Pain is the main problem and it may occur at rest, but there may also be numbness in the arm and hand and loss of muscle power	Aspirin and related drugs for the pain. Trapped nerves may have to be freed by surgery

Q I have had both the cartilages removed from my left knee. Am I likely to get osteoarthritis as a result?

A There is no certainty that you will get the disease (though do remember that half the population over 50 have some symptoms). However, people who have had their cartilages removed do have more osteoarthritis of the knee than people who haven't. Moreover, the chances of this occurring are increased if you get a knee injury where a cartilage is torn. This may lead to abnormalities in knee function, which in turn may cause osteoarthritis.

In order that you can avoid risking a repeated injury to your knee, you may have to give up contact sports if you play them.

Q I have osteoarthritis and I find that if I sit down for an hour, my joints seize up. Is this a common thing to happen with the disease?

A Yes. People with arthritis do tend to feel stiff after they have not been moving their joints for a while. In one of the other common sorts of arthritis – rheumatoid arthritis – affected patients frequently feel stiff in the mornings, and this also happens in osteoarthritis. The stiffness only lasts about a quarter of an hour in osteoarthritis, whereas in patients with rheumatoid arthritis, this symptom may go on for a much longer period of time.

Q Who is more likely to get osteoarthritis – men or women and does it affect them differently?

A Osteoarthritis is a disease that particularly affects the elderly, and since women live to a greater age than men, it would appear that more women suffer from it. Among the younger age groups, men and women are almost equally affected, with men perhaps sometimes slightly more so.

In spite of this, the two sexes tend to get the disease in different joints. In men it is more common for the hips to be involved, while in women it is the hands, knees and the base of the thumb.

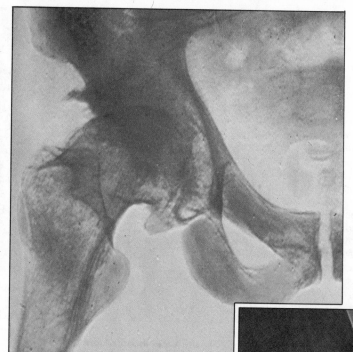

These X-rays of an osteoarthritic hip (left) and knee (below) show how the disease has affected the joints. Normally bones are lined with cartilage and joints are protected. Here the cartilage caps have worn away and because the bone ends bear directly on each other, they too are worn away by movement. Pain and stiffness result.

CNRI/Vision International

due to some problem in the nervous system. Since the sensation of pain is interrupted, the patient may injure a joint repeatedly and not be aware of it.

However the fact remains that there is no obvious cause in the majority of patients with the disease.

Symptoms

The main symptom of osteoarthritis is pain. This can vary in severity from a dull ache in an affected joint to an excruciating pain on movement which may make patients practically immobile. Usually the pain from an osteoarthritic joint is worse during movement. There may also be pain of a duller aching character when the joint is at rest. This pain is thought to result from the disorganization of the way that the veins drain blood from the joint: rest pain may well be due to the joint being congested with blood.

The pain tends to become steadily worse, although the severity of the joint's involvement is not always a good indication of the degree of pain. Further, the pain may not actually be felt in the joint involved: it is common for osteoarthritis of the hip to come to light as a result of pain in the knee on the same side, or in the back.

Osteoarthritis also causes stiffness. This is usually worse in the morning, but tends to get better within a few minutes. The affected joints may also swell in some cases.

As the disease progresses, there may be considerable deformity in the joints. Badly affected hips and knees creak;

doctors call this crepitus. The range of movement decreases as the arthritis progresses, and in some cases the joint may become almost fixed.

Osteoarthritis may affect one joint in the body or it may affect several. If only one joint is involved, it is likely to be a big joint such as the knee or hip. Occasionally the only joint involved is where the palm and wrist meet on the thumb side. Other common sites for multiple affected joints are the hand and the spine.

Dangers

Although very unpleasant, osteoarthritis is not often dangerous. However serious problems can arise when the disease affects the spine in the neck, causing pain and stiffness. This condition is known as cervical spondylosis. Three problems can arise from this; the first is pain and stiffness of the neck.

The second and third, which are serious but rare, arise from attempts of the bone to repair itself, leading to bone overgrowth. Pressure on the blood vessels to the lower part of the brain will cut off the blood supply, leading to blackouts and dizziness when looking upwards or round to the side. Pressure on the spinal cord or its nerves will lead to weakness in both the arms and legs.

Treatment
Painkilling drugs are the best treatment to stop pain and to reduce any inflammation. Aspirin is the most favoured, but other drugs can be taken where patients cannot tolerate it. Supportive measures include using a walking stick for cases of osteoarthritis of the knee and hip.

Joint replacement surgery is used in severely affected cases, resulting in a dramatic lessening of pain, and improvement of joint movement. The most successful operation is on the hip joint, although there has been some progress in knee joint replacement.

Apart from joint replacement, an operation called an osteotomy, where the bones on either side of a joint are remodelled, can be of great value as it improves the way the joint carries weight. This operation tends to be used in younger patients, since no one is certain how long replaced joints last, and there is always the option of replacing the joint at some later stage.

Finally the joint can be completely fused so that it cannot move and cannot cause pain. Although this sounds drastic, it can be extremely successful in some patients. It can bring tremendous pain relief, often without much loss of function in the affected limb, which probably was fairly stiff in the first place.

Outlook
Once osteoarthritis occurs, it will not disappear. However most people have very few symptoms from the disease. Where symptoms are a problem, they can be greatly relieved by drugs in the majority of cases.

Surgical treatment can also bring about tremendous relief of pain, especially in the hip, although in other joints this form of treatment should be regarded as a last resort.

Hip replacement

The head of the femur is removed, holes are drilled and plastic cement is pushed in.

A prosthetic ball and stem is inserted into the femur, and held in place by the cement.

Stem and head are rejoined and traction is applied to maintain the position of the leg.

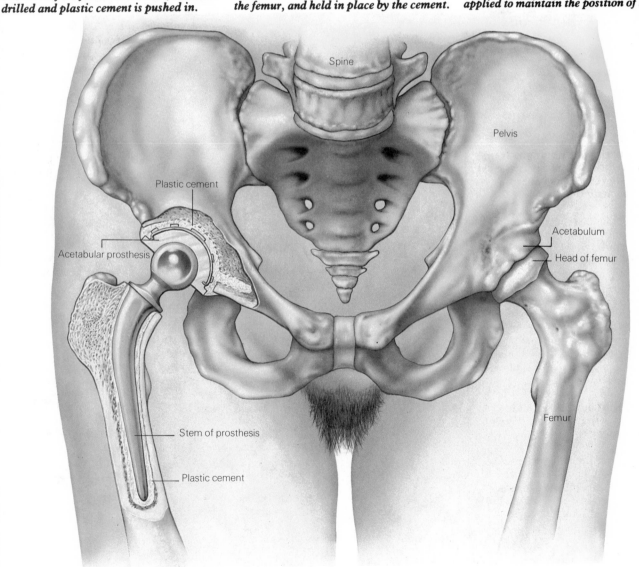

Spine

Pelvis

Plastic cement

Acetabular prosthesis

Acetabulum

Head of femur

Stem of prosthesis

Plastic cement

Femur

Frank Kennard

Osteomyelitis

Q My daughter has got osteomyelitis. Is it possible that the infection can spread from the bone to the surrounding tissue?

A It is much more usual for infection to spread from the bone to the surrounding tissue than for it to happen the other way round. What usually occurs is that infection breaks through the fibrous coating of the bone into the surrounding muscle and then penetrates the skin forming a sinus which will not heal until the infection is completely eradicated. However, in rare instances tuberculosis may spread in the opposite way – in other words from the lung tissue into the bone.

Q Could osteomyelitis possibly lead to developing cancer of the bone?

A Yes, but it is an extremely rare complication. However, it is recognized that bone infection can lead to the development of osteosarcoma which is one type of bone cancer.

Q I have recently suffered from osteomyelitis of the leg. Will I be able to return to my normal sporting activities?

A Yes. Modern antibiotics, in combination with surgical draining procedures, can now completely cure osteomyelitis. Provided that all the dead bone is removed, all the damage is repaired completely within the course of about six months and full sporting activities can then be resumed. It is important to remember that complete bed-rest is essential while the infection is in its most virulent stage.

Q My son has a boil on his leg. Is it likely that he could develop osteomyelitis?

A No. Since the introduction of antibiotics a boil can be effectively treated in the early stages and it is extremely unlikely that the bacteria would spread through the bloodstream to infect other areas of his body.

At one time osteomyelitis – bone infection – could have had very serious consequences like amputation of an infected limb. But nowadays, antibiotics and modern medical care usually give a complete recovery.

Osteomyelitis is an infection of the bone by bacteria or fungus. The infection can be acute, which is sudden and severe, or chronic which is gradual. It is introduced into the bone through compound fractures, infected wounds or after surgery.

Children under the age of 12 are particularly at risk and before antibiotics the disease could cause bone deformation and lameness.

Causes

Bacteria can enter the bone during surgery when the skin has been cut or as a complication of a compound fracture when bone breaks through the skin, or else infection is carried from inflammation elsewhere via the blood to lodge in the bones. This is known as hematogenous spread and accounts for about 90 per cent of the cases of osteomyelitis.

Structure of a long bone

Bacteria which have been introduced into the blood can get trapped in the end arteries of the growing ends of long bones and cause infection, pain and inflammation.

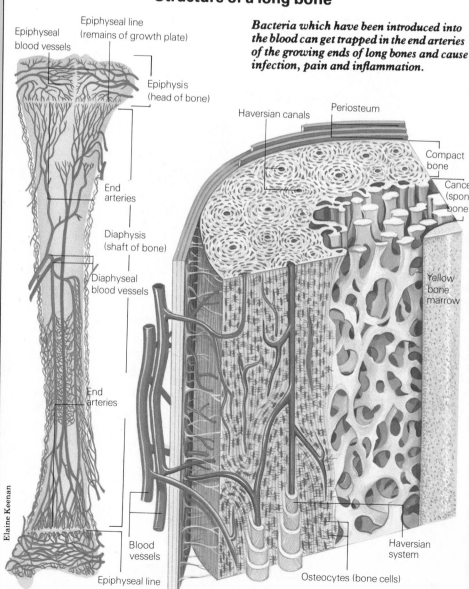

Epiphyseal blood vessels

Epiphyseal line (remains of growth plate)

Epiphysis (head of bone)

End arteries

Diaphysis (shaft of bone)

Diaphyseal blood vessels

End arteries

Blood vessels

Epiphyseal line

Haversian canals

Periosteum

Compact bone

Cance (spon bone

Yellow bone marrow

Haversian system

Osteocytes (bone cells)

Elaine Keenan

A large majority of cases of osteomyelitis are caused by the bacteria known as staphylococcus. This bacteria is often carried to the bone by the blood from skin infections such as carbuncles or boils. Rarer bacteria may affect people with poor resistance to infection, such as newborn babies and people with blood diseases like leukaemia.

Symptoms

The first symptoms are pain, inflammation and the formation of pus in the affected limb. However, because the bone is a rigid structure the swelling is contained. The production of pus causes a rapid rise in pressure in the bone causing severe pain which may develop quite dramatically; sometimes overnight. Vomiting is sometimes experienced and there is, in addition, always the symptom of an accompanying fever.

The infection particularly affects the growing ends of the long bones around the knee joint and around the elbow joint in the arms. The reason for this is that the blood vessels here do not run into veins—they are known as end arteries. This means that any bacteria finding their way to bone get filtered here and stick. Once the bone infection is established the pressure within the bone slows the circulation of the blood so that areas of bone may die. Eventually the pus may pass out of the bone through a skin opening—a sinus.

Dangers

Before antibiotics were introduced acute osteomyelitis proved fatal in 50 per cent of cases. This was because the infection spread in the blood to involve other organs like the lungs.

Now the main danger is that chronic osteomyelitis may develop. The problem is that inflammation continues with swelling and pus, the bone is weakened and the infection may become acute again.

Different types of osteomyelitis

The tuberculosis bacteria can also infect bone and when it does it attacks the back bones by direct spread from the lungs. The progression is slow but bone is eaten away, leaving behind normal discs which form the fibrous padding between the vertebrae. When sufficient bone has been destroyed the weight of the body is no longer supported and the spine then crumbles resulting in a bent back. This sharp angulation created at the centre of the back is known as kyphosis. Sufferers of this condition are commonly called hunchbacks.

Tuberculosis infections can normally be diagnosed by an accurate X-ray.

In the USA infection with a fungus called North American blastomycosis occurs. This does not respond to antibiotics and a special anti-fungal agent needs to be used. Another fungus called actinomycosis causes cases in Asia.

Treatment

Early treatment of acute osteomyelitis is essential, because once areas of dead bone have formed, chronic osteomyelitis is likely to follow.

Admission to hospital will be necessary. The doctors will take blood samples to try to identify which bacteria is causing the infection. Antiobiotics will be given intravenously at first, and later by mouth. Many people will need an operation consisting of drilling small holes in the bone. This relieves the pressure caused by the infection, and also allows the doctors to test the pus to make sure that the bacteria causing the infection will be killed by the antibiotics they are currently using in order to treat the patient's condition.

If there is chronic osteomyelitis, antibiotics alone cannot cure the infection. An operation will be necessary to remove all the infected and dead bone. If the chronic osteomyelitis is extensive, this may mean amputation of the affected limb.

Outlook

With early treatment there is now a good chance that a full recovery will be made from acute osteomyelitis.

The onset of osteomyelitis can be very sudden causing extreme pain in the affected joint. Prompt diagnosis and early treatment is essential.

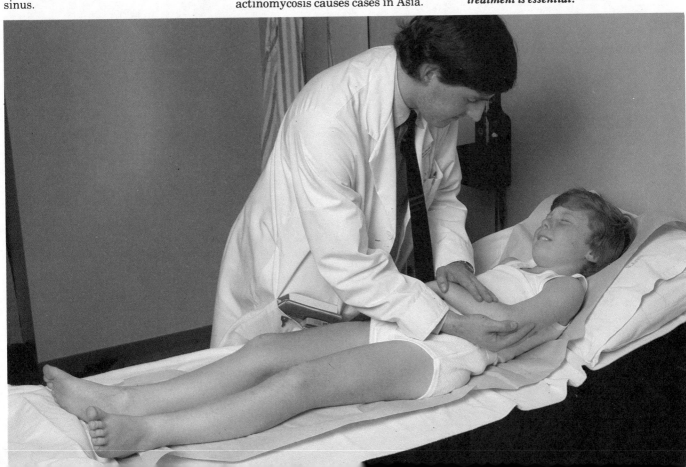

Osteopathy

Q Are chiropracters and osteopaths the same?

A No, there are differences. Although many of the services and treatments are similar, chiropracters use direct adjustment of the spine while osteopaths use massage and manipulation more frequently. In the US, chiropracters are more familiar to most people.

Q How can I find an osteopath if my doctor is unable to recommend one to me?

A If your doctor cannot help, treatment from a qualified osteopath may be obtained by consulting one of the professional osteopathic associations. Their services can be found in traditional hospitals and in clinics or hospitals set up by osteopaths.

Q Are all osteopaths medically qualified?

A Usually, yes, and practitioners who have completed a formal medical training will be identified by the letters 'D.O.' after their names, often followed by letters that signify membership of a professional organization.

Q My doctor says that my low back pain is from a 'slipped disc'. Could osteopathy help?

A There are many causes of pain in the low back and while a prolapsed ('slipped') disc is sometimes responsible, the term is often used by doctors in a more general way to explain symptoms to patients. A genuine prolapse will probably require a period of bed-rest to allow healing to occur, but skilful manipulation can often reduce the pressure on the nerve root which is causing the pain. Many cases diagnosed as 'slipped discs' are in reality strains or sprains of the muscles, ligaments or joint capsules of the spine and in these instances, a course of osteopathic treatment can effectively relieve the symptoms.

The art of manipulation and massage – osteopathy – has been practised since ancient times. Today it is becoming more accepted as a treatment which can achieve success where conventional medicine seems to fail.

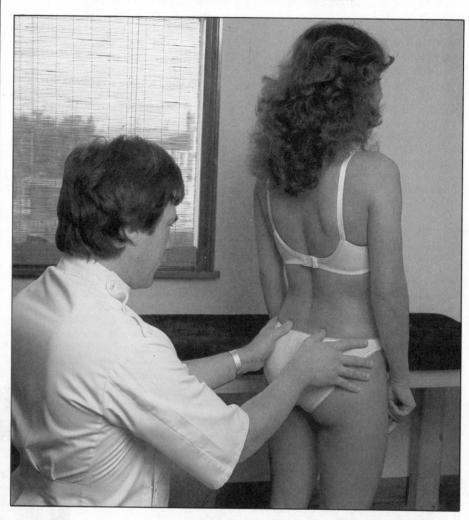

Osteopathy is a system of medicine which concentrates its diagnosis and treatment essentially on the bones, muscles, ligaments and joints in the body. At the same time, however, it is a therapy which recognizes all parts of the body and takes into account people's health, lifestyle, environment, diet and stress factors in regard to treatment.

The osteopath is a highly trained practitioner who uses his hands to treat the body when illness arises; to restore body control mechanisms; relieve pain and discomfort; and improve the mobility of every joint in the body.

Although massage and manipulation have existed since ancient times, the art and science of osteopathy originated in the USA in the late 19th century. The founder, Andrew Taylor Still, had

Osteopathic treatment begins with a thorough diagnosis and a structural assessment of the patient. The situation is reviewed on each treatment session.

qualified as a doctor but like many of his contemporaries he was deeply sceptical of many of the methods then in use. He had begun to develop a consuming interest in the structure of the body during his childhood; and he chose 'osteopathy' (bone disease) as the name for his system of healing to underline the principle that 'structure governs function'. Although this was doubted by the medical profession of his day, modern research has lent some truth to the principle. The self-regulating activities which keep numerous body functions within proper limits (homeostasis) are closely related to the structural components by different reflexes of the nervous system. By working to bring back to normal the relationships of joints (especially of the spine), muscles, ligaments and connective tissue, the osteopath is able to produce far-reaching, and sometimes dramatic, effects for the whole body.

Scope of osteopathy

Most people who consult an osteopath do so because they have pain and restricted movement somewhere – often in the lower back, or the neck, or perhaps the shoulder. These injuries arise for many different reasons ranging from accidents to rheumatism. The fact that the hands of the osteopath can often resolve these problems faster and more completely than bed-rest and drugs has assured the

popularity and continued development and growth of the osteopathic profession as a respected practice.

Medicine divides diseases into the principal categories of 'organic' and 'functional'. Organic illnesses are those in which destruction or permanent alteration of some body tissue or system occurs, for instance: tuberculosis, cancer, diseases of bone, cirrhosis of the liver or coronary artery disease. Functional illnesses occur when the body is not working properly, either because of infection, changes in blood pressure, or by recurring symptoms of migraine or asthma for example. Many illnesses called 'psychosomatic' are given this label because no obvious medical reason can be found for the disorder. The presence of anxiety, stress, and emotional

or personality problems often accompanies these disorders with the resulting symptoms of muscular tension, disturbed circulation, and altered nerve and hormonal supply. Osteopathy, by treating these associated symptoms manually, has a constructive and powerful role to play in the healing process.

Osteopathic treatment is suitable for people of all ages, male or female. It is especially applicable to growing children, since if potential disorders are detected and treated at this stage, future disability can be prevented. Strains, sprains, falls and other minor injuries generally are only painful for a time, but long-term effects caused by muscular and ligamentous shortening, fibrosis and minor derangements in joints are common. Eventually, lack of exercise,

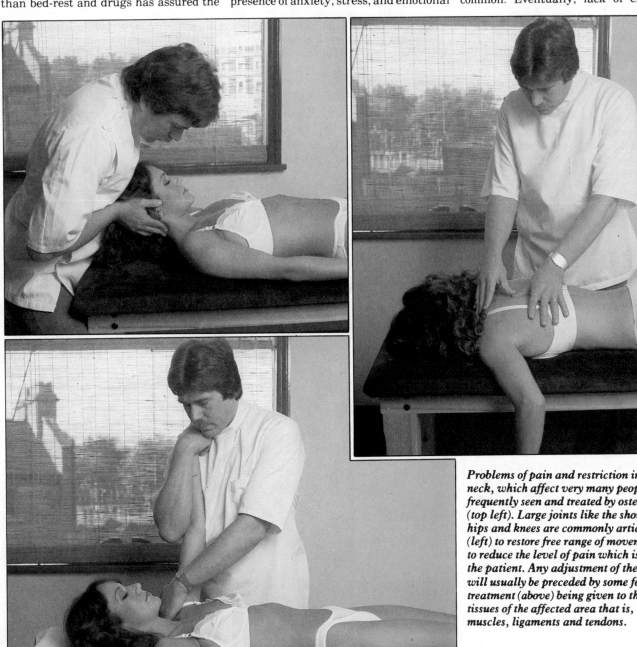

Problems of pain and restriction in the neck, which affect very many people, are frequently seen and treated by osteopaths (top left). Large joints like the shoulders, hips and knees are commonly articulated (left) to restore free range of movement and to reduce the level of pain which is felt by the patient. Any adjustment of the spine will usually be preceded by some form of treatment (above) being given to the soft tissues of the affected area that is, the muscles, ligaments and tendons.

Q What causes the 'pops' when the osteopath adjusts my spine?

A Each vertebra in the spine has four bony projections which form joints with adjacent vertebrae. Each of these joints is enclosed by a fibrous capsule, with synovial fluid inside as a lubricant. When the spine is manipulated, the joint surfaces are forced apart, which disturbs the pressure equilibrium inside the joint capsule. The resulting pop is similar in principle to cracking the knuckles, or suddenly pulling your finger out of your mouth pressing the inside of one cheek as children do. The sound is louder because it goes along the bones of the spine.

Q My 14-year-old son has developed a curvature of the spine. Can osteopathic treatment help him?

A It depends on the reason for the curvature. If it is caused by an accident or poor posture, then a complete cure can be expected. However, a few children develop a more severe curvature (scoliosis) which is hereditary. Regular osteopathic treatment during the growing phase can usually reduce the degree of curvature, but surgical splinting of the spine is sometimes the only answer.

Q The osteopath I consulted for low back pain has advised me to have all my shoes fitted with a higher heel on one foot. Why it this?

A You may have a primary short leg, that is, the bones in one leg are actually shorter than the other. This is fairly common, either as a result of an earlier fracture, or because the bones grew at different rates for some reason. The effect of this is to unbalance the pelvis, forcing the spine to bend to one side and form compensatory curves. The unequal pressures and muscular tensions of this posture can cause strains and consequent backache. Although most spines are sufficiently flexible to adapt to a small difference, a heel lift or specially modified shoe may be necessary to level the pelvis and remove the strain caused by the imbalance.

obesity, increasing age, or a subsequent injury can reveal these weaknesses. Increased susceptibility to injury or the onset of arthritis are common developments of these earlier problems if they are left untreated.

Osteopaths do not see their therapy as a substitute for medicine or surgery in diseases where these methods are clearly more effective. However, in the treatment of muscle and bone disorders, functional illness, and chronic diseases that affect the structure of the body, osteopathic diagnosis and treatment are often effective where other methods have been tried and have failed.

Training
Osteopaths undergo a four-year training in specialized colleges after first studying the biological sciences. They study medical disciplines including anatomy, physiology, pathology, biochemistry and neurology, as well as the specialized

subjects of osteopathic diagnosis and treatment. The distinctive feature of the training is the development of great sensitivity of the hands – an essential requirement for proper diagnosis – and the corresponding artistry and subtlety in the application through treatment to the body.

Diagnosis of the problem can involve initial X-rays, blood and urine tests and referral to specific specialists.

Theory and practice
The various body systems function normally by extremely sophisticated processes of communication and control. The role of the muscles and bones is much greater than simply providing support and a framework for the body. The muscles for instance, besides enabling physical work and self-expression also affect bone structure and posture, circulation, metabolism and hormone balance. Osteopathy is specifically con-

cerned with the ways in which disturbances and injuries of a mechanical nature can influence other body processes and contribute to poor health through all these control systems.

A central part of this theory has been called the 'osteopathic lesion'. In medical terms a lesion is a disturbance of the structure or function of the body, such as a wound, tumour or chemical abnormality. In osteopathic practice, a lesion is a more complex and subtle disturbance which may appear as a source of pain or discomfort, and often goes quite unnoticed by the patient, or by normal medical examination.

The osteopathic lesion – discovered by careful touch examination and specific tests – may be an area of contracted muscle or a shortened ligament anywhere in the body, and frequently occurs as a change in normal joint movement in the spinal column. The vertebrae themselves are passive structures, and are pushed or pulled about by the forces of gravity, trauma and muscular or ligamentous action. The distinctive contribution of osteopathic medicine is to seek out and then correct these disturbances by manual methods, supplemented where necessary by other therapies – especially change in diet and environment. By resolving these disturbances, local pain or discomfort from muscle spasm or irritation of nerve roots is relieved, and altered circulation is achieved, along with beneficial effects for the health of the person.

From the osteopathic point of view, the spinal lesion is often the largest single contributing factor in this vicious circle of functional and organic disorder, and the correcting influences of manipulation are applied to restore the natural defences and to encourage the tendency of the body to restore body controls, thereby restoring the patient's good health and his or her general well-being.

Treatment

A typical session lasts about 20 to 30 minutes. Once the cause of pain or illness has been determined, the osteopath will decide if manipulation is safe and desirable, and if so, what type of treatment to apply. Frequently, any specific spinal manipulation is preceded by soft tissue work, massage, stretching and putting the joints through their range of movement. Some osteopaths practise a specialized form of manipulation applied to the head and upper neck (cranial osteopathy). This is a gentle treatment and is particularly useful for young children and for treating functional disorders like migraine, sinusitis and visual disturbances.

The number of sessions needed varies widely among individuals but most osteopaths prefer to give a course of treatment sufficient to resolve the main problem, improve general mobility and health and to prevent against further problems in the future.

Dangers

There are a number of diseases and conditions for which manipulation is undesirable, or even dangerous. The skill and experience of the practitioner should determine whether spinal disc herniation or prolapses, osteoarthritis or severe sciatica are attempted. However, tuberculosis, malignancy, fractures, acute arthritis, various diseases of bone and severe cases of prolapsed discs which cause neurological symptoms should not be manipulated under any circumstances. A qualified osteopath is able to detect these conditions and make appropriate referrals, but others may not. Repeated manipulation of the same joints is inadvisable, since this can lead to stretching of the ligaments and instability of the joint.

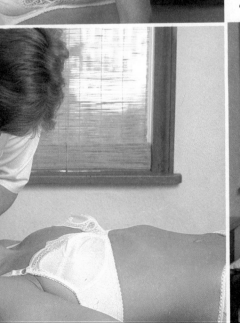

A lifting technique (far left below) for correcting abnormal conditions of the dorsal spine – mid to upper area – is commonly used in osteopathy. The movement (far left) is used for correcting abnormalities in the same region of the spine and allows specific joint restrictions to be freed painlessly. Correcting problems in the vital area of the neck (below centre) can often resolve problems like migraine and poor vision as well as removing the source of pain and discomfort. The osteopath also uses a 'sitting correction' (left) for the patient's neck and back area, using the head and neck as a lever. If problems in this area are not resolved a 'dowager's hump' may result. Low back pain is a very common condition – if the problem is caused by muscular trouble or joint malfunction, manipulation (below) can generally greatly alleviate the pain and discomfort.

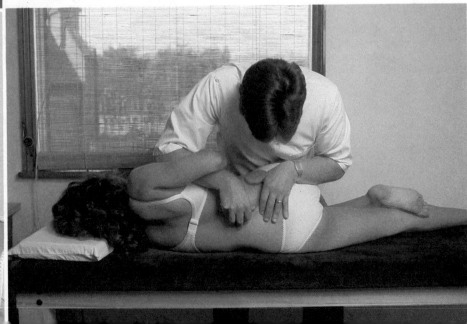

Osteoporosis

Q My mother has developed a humped back. It seems to have come gradually since her 70th birthday. She calls it her 'dowager's hump' and says it's not worth bothering about because it doesn't hurt. Is she right? And what caused it?

A It is the result of osteoporosis—when the bones become smaller, lighter and less robust than normal. Over the years this has meant some of the bones in her spine have become squashed, and that others have collapsed into a wedge shape, so that the spine has bent into the hump shape you describe.

Your mother is right not to worry about it: there is no danger to life, and severe cases are rare. It often causes no pain.

Q I've heard I can avoid osteoporosis if I drink plenty of milk. Is this true?

A Although some of the constituents of milk are essential for the growth of bone, milk cannot prevent osteoporosis which is a condition of old age and its accompanying changes in the balance of the body's hormones or chemical messengers. So, by all means, drink plenty of milk, but don't expect it to work wonders.

Q I've heard that women on hormone replacement therapy do not develop osteoporosis. Is this true, and if so, why?

A Hormone replacement therapy is given to women who suffer particularly badly from the 'change of life' and involves giving the hormone oestrogen, which the body stops producing naturally at the menopause. It is indeed thought that lack of oestrogen is a cause of osteoporosis, and hormone replacement does seem to reverse the condition to some extent.

However, you are only likely to be given hormone replacement therapy if you are having particularly severe menopausal problems; giving hormones 'artificially' can have side-effects.

This condition – unusually light and fragile bones – affects mainly the vertebrae and is, in most cases, an exaggerated effect of ageing rather than a disease.

The bones in our bodies are not, as some people imagine, dead, but living material which is constantly changing. When such change involves a loss of bone, it is described as osteoporosis.

Causes
The most common cause is in fact age. From middle age onwards, everyone's bones become lighter. This change is more marked in women after the menopause or 'change of life', but in both men and women lighter bones are normal in old age. It is only when an excessive amount of bone is lost that symptoms of osteoporosis arise.

There are other, more complicated causes of osteoporosis, most of which are rare. In these cases, the loss of bone is usually a result of drastic changes in the body brought about by another illness. In this case the osteoporosis is described as secondary, since it is an effect of the initial, or primary illness which will disappear if that illness is cured. Many of these rare causes are diseases of the hormonal system.

There is, however, one relatively common secondary cause, generally described as immobilization, and simply meaning that the patient is 'laid up' for some reason. Thus osteoporosis is often seen in the bones of a single limb which cannot be moved because of pain, paralysis or a broken – fractured – bone.

Symptoms
The condition may cause no symptoms at all or alternatively, it may give rise to bone pain and backache.

Advanced cases suffer from deformities such as loss of height or a bent spine. The bones will tend to break rather easily, even as a result of some minor accident or trivial strain.

The commonest fracture associated with the condition is collapse of one of the vertebrae (small bones) of the spine. This may not hurt, or it may give rise to severe pain over that bone, which incidentally tends to improve without treatment over the next two or three months. In the long term, several of these fractures may occur and as a result the spine becomes shortened and bent.

The other common fracture site is the hip, which is more than usually vulnerable in old people whose poor balance and

The elderly are prone to osteoporosis. The weakened bones can result in minor deformities or cause falls.

How osteoporosis affects the spine

Wedge fractures

Vertebra

The vertebrae are easily fractured and often become wedge shaped as a result

Intervertebral disc

The discs erode the vertebral surfaces, making them concave

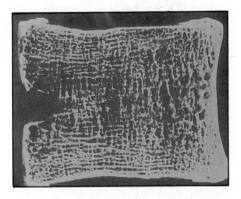

This X-ray of a normal vertebra shows bone with both a normal calcium content and a regular structure.

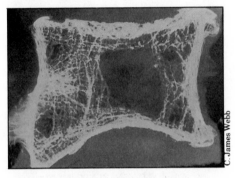

Osteoporosis in this vertebra shows up clearly. The affected areas look blacker than normal bone would.

The vertebrae in a spine affected by osteoporosis are easily fractured and often become wedge shaped. The intervertebral discs erode the surfaces of the vertebrae, making them concave. The net result is a shortening of the spine and the characteristic 'humped' look.

The back troubles associated with the condition may affect the nerves leading from the spine to the limbs, giving pain and weakness. In the most advanced cases, the back can become bent almost double, and there may be considerable breathing difficulty.

Treatment
The aim of treatment is to keep the patient mobile. Exercise promotes strong bones, and prevents their deterioration, so following a fracture the patient is encouraged to get moving as soon as possible.

In order to give the bones the best conditions for growth, an ample protein diet is advised, and the raw materials for bone, calcium and vitamin D, are given. Several drugs have been tried, as yet without proven benefits.

Outlook
We will all, to some extent, suffer from this benign condition as we get older, and most of us will never know we have it. In a few unlucky individuals there will be pain, broken bones or disability, but with careful management, and continuing research into treatments and possible cures, the outlook for them, too, is improving steadily.

general stiffness make them liable to fall. If an elderly patient has osteoporosis, a relatively minor blow – or, as the doctors say, trauma – will often be enough to break the hip-bone.

Diagnosis
The diagnosis of osteoporosis is confirmed with X-rays and blood tests. Often an X-ray taken for some other reason will reveal osteoporosis of which the patient is unaware. On the processed X-ray film, the affected bones look blacker and hidden fractures may be found.

The blood tests are done mainly to check whether the patient has other diseases that have similar symptoms, or whether there is a disease which can cause secondary osteoporosis, such as thyrotoxicosis – an overactive thyroid.

Dangers
This is not a dangerous condition, and in itself it is never fatal. Its worst consequence, in the occasional really severe case, is disability. Repeated fractures may confine a patient who is suffering from osteoporosis to a wheelchair.

Otitis

Thanks to antibiotics, otitis – infection of the ears – should not be dangerous these days. However, it is still important to seek early treatment, especially as this will help prevent recurrence of ear problems.

Parts of the ear

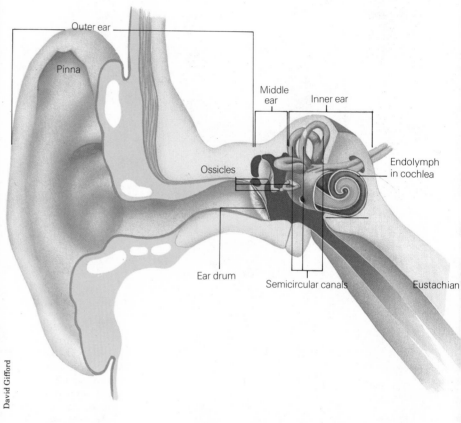

David Gifford

Each ear has three parts which combine to make it the organ of both hearing and balance. The outer ear, or visible part, receives sound waves which are transmitted via the ear-drum to the middle ear. Here they are amplified by a series of three bones called the ossicles, before passing through another membrane into the inner ear. In this compartment sound vibrations are converted into electrical impulses which reach the brain along a pair of nerves, to be interpreted, or perceived there, as sound.

There are membranes between the three parts of the ear which help to ward off infection, particularly from the inner ear which must always be protected. The process of transmitting information in the form of sound can be interrupted by infection. The three types of infection relate directly to the three parts of the ear, and are called respectively otitis externa, otitis media and otitis interna.

Otitis externa

Otitis externa is inflammation of the skin of the outer ear by bacteria or fungi. It usually arises when the ear is not dried after getting wet, or if the skin is very sensitive and prone to eczema. The canal leading towards the middle ear may also be affected if the wax in it becomes irritated, which may occur if the ear is explored with a sharp instrument, such as a matchstick or paper clip.

The ear may become red and itchy, sometimes with a watery discharge, although the condition itself may not be very painful. Drops and ointment are useful in clearing up mild cases of inflammation, but where infection is severe and painful, antibiotics taken by mouth are the best treatment, especially since it may not only be the outer ear which is affected. It is always important to remember that any unskilled treatment of ears is extremely unwise.

infection to the mastoid cells or the skull cavity, which in the past was a serious complication called mastoiditis. Where a virus is the cause of otitis media antibiotics are of course not given.

It is a very common condition of babies and toddlers who may not even complain of earache but simply feel unwell with perhaps a temperature. For this reason doctors always examine the ears of young children who have a fever.

Chronic otitis media

Occasionally the problem recurs when infection enters the middle ear through the discharging hole in the drum. Earache persists, and there may be a slight discharge of pus. Impaired or painful hearing may ensue as the ear-drum and ossicles become scarred, hence the need for prompt treatment to prevent this.

With careful cleansing the infection can often be controlled, but where the bone is affected surgery may be necessary. Serious defects in the drum may be repaired by grafting once the infection has completely cleared up.

Otitis interna

Otitis interna is now very rare, but may still arise if middle ear infection has been allowed to spread, resulting in deafness and giddiness. Treatment should therefore be sought early, before any permanent damage can be done.

Swimming is best avoided where there is any ear infection. A simple tuning-fork test (below) will reveal any reduction in hearing due to fluid in the middle ear.

Otitis media

Otitis media is most likely to result from a bacterial or viral infection of the nose and throat. This reaches the ear along the Eustachian tube, the passage leading from the back of the nose to the middle ear. Such complications are very common in children, and may follow an illness like measles, tonsillitis or common cold.

Acute otitis media can cause violent earache and fever, accompanied by muffled hearing. This is due to a build-up of fluid in the middle ear, which normally contains only air. Where bacterial not viral infection is suspected, antibiotics are given otherwise the earache persists until the ear-drum perforates to discharge the pus. Sometimes the ear-drum has to be drained surgically to drain off pus but once the infection has cleared up the drum heals and there should be no further trouble.

A doctor should be consulted at once in any suspected case of middle ear infection. Sulphonamides and other antibiotics nowadays prevent the spread of

N. Shah

Out-patients

Q My mother has just been in the hospital with a heart attack. Will she have to go on visiting the out-patient department when she is better?

A In the UK, probably yes. In the US, however, many people are treated privately and these patients will be followed by their specialist in his office rather than going to an out-patient department. If the patient has been cared for in a university teaching hospital, however, they probably will return there for a follow-up as in the UK.

Q I have difficulty getting around, and I cannot afford a taxi. How will I get to the hospital?

A If there is no one in your family who can take you perhaps there is a neighbour that you can ask. Your doctor may be able to put you in touch with a charitable organization that offers such a service, or your local church may be able to help. Do remember that groups such as these will be helping others and this may involve your waiting while everyone finishes with their appointments.

Q Can I take a friend to the hospital with me?

A Certainly you can. The specialist may allow you to bring your friend in with you when you have your appointment, but you should always ask first.

Q If I am late for an appointment, will the specialist still see me, or will I have to wait for another appointment?

A That depends on how late you are. Most specialists will see several patients in a morning or afternoon session, so that if you arrive before the end of a session you will probably be seen. If you are very late, on the other hand, the specialist probably has commitments elsewhere, so that he is unlikely to be able to see you. You can always telephone the hospital if you think you are going to be late, and the staff will advise you on the best thing to do.

When we think of a hospital, most of us imagine wards with long lines of beds. In fact, most of the day-to-day work of modern district general hospital is generally carried out i the out-patients department.

When you visit out-patients you, and whoever you're accompanying, will have to wait your turn. Some hospitals are far-sighted enough to provide toys to make the time pass pleasantly for your children.

John Moss/Colorfic!

When your doctor feels that you should have the benefit of the advice and treatment of a hospital specialist, he will usually recommend that you see one in that part of the hospital out-patient department where that particular specialist holds his session. You will need to take with you a letter from your doctor to the specialist; this will detail the condition that needs to be investigated and treated.

The specialist then has all the resources of the hospital to enable him to investigate your case and to treat you— once, of course, he has made a clear diagnosis. Many cases can be sorted out without the patient ever needing to stay in a hospital ward, although people who are referred to one of the surgeons at the hospital may need to be admitted for an operation at some point.

Use of out-patients departments

There has been a great expansion in the use of out-patient facilities in all hospitals in recent years and nowadays every effort is made to avoid admitting people to the wards unless it is absolutely necessary. Not only is this better for the patients, who do not have their lives disrupted by a stay in the hospital, and less expensive, it is also better for the hospital itself—keeping people in a ward means all sorts of services have to be provided on a 24-hour, seven days a week basis.

Most large hospitals have a physiotherapy department which out-patients convalescing at home can attend. This is a vital post-operative service.

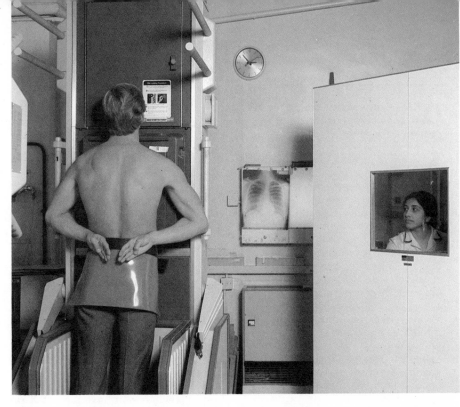

Some people need complicated tests and procedures carried out even though they are not ill enough to require the level of nursing care that the staff of an ordinary surgical or medical ward provide. To help in this sort of situation, many hospitals have created special wards which are half way between an ordinary ward and the out-patient department. These may vary from the sort of 'investigation unit' that takes in patients for tests first thing in the morning and then closes at five or six o'clock every night, to 'five-day wards' which are open 24 hours a day during the week but

You may have to visit the X-ray department as an out-patient—in some hospitals, even before you have seen a specialist.

cut the cost to the hospital by closing at the weekends. The sort of tests that these wards carry out could include all forms of endoscopy (see pp 455-6): for these, sedation instead of a full-scale general anaesthetic is used and so a patient can go home the same evening. In other cases a whole series of blood tests can be carried out—for example, investigating the control of the level of blood sugar in a diabetic by measuring it every couple of hours during the course of an entire day.

Out-patient investigations

Nearly all the investigations that are carried out on patients in the ward can also be carried out in out-patients. So many cases are sent for blood tests from the departments of an ordinary general hospital that there is nearly always a special area in the hospital, often near the out-patients area, where specially trained technicians take all the blood specimens: they are sent from there to the pathology laboratory for analysis.

Tests can also be carried out on specimens of urine that are taken in the hospital—or you might be asked to bring from home some special specimen for examination, like a specimen of sputum from those with a cough, or a specimen of feces in people with bowel disorders.

Just as the laboratory carries out tests on out-patients, so too does the X-ray department. If you are sent to see a specialist you may well be asked to go to the X-ray department as a result of your visit. Many of the more simple X-rays can

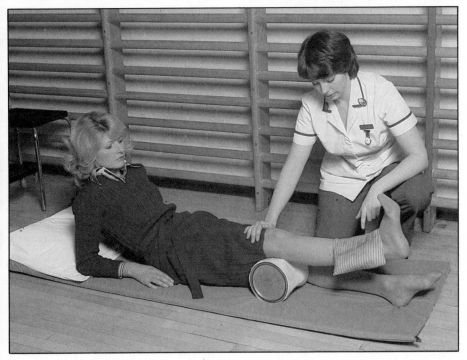

Q **If I feel unwell at work, can I go to the nearest hospital out-patient department?**

A No. You should telephone your family doctor. Hospital out-patients departments are for people receiving short-term or continuous treatment from particular specialists.

If you have an urgent problem, then you can go to the Accident and Emergency Department (casualty department) of the nearest hospital. However you should not do this unless it is a genuine accident or emergency. These departments are always very busy. You must also remember that the doctors and nurses decide on the order in which patients are seen on the basis of the severity of the medical condition, not on a first-come-first-served basis, so you might have to wait.

All in all, the best thing to do is to see your own family doctor unless you have a really urgent problem like a badly bleeding wound.

Q **I have been to out-patients at my local hospital three times now, and it has been a different doctor each time. Why does this happen?**

A There are many possible reasons for this. The doctors there will usually consist of a specialist and junior colleagues. In many cases it is usual for the specialist to see a new case and then to hand the patient over to another doctor. In addition, junior doctors may change rather frequently and move on to a new post every six months. But you can soon expect to see the same doctor more or less regularly.

Q **If I am too ill to go to the out-patients department, but my doctor doesn't think I need to be admitted to a hospital, is there any other way that he can get a specialist's opinion?**

A In some cases a specialist may be willing to visit you at home. However, it might be impossible for him to come in reasonable time, for example, or he may feel, after discussing the problem with your GP, that you have to be admitted to a hospital.

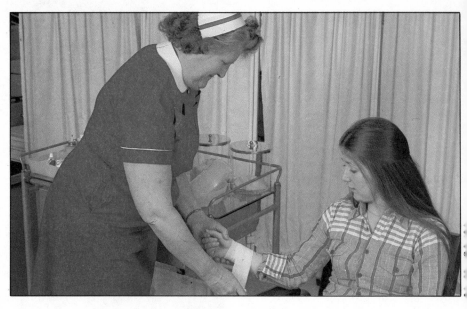

be carried out there and then, and you may go straight back to the specialist with the X-ray films for him or her to have a look at. (There are even some hospitals where you have a chest X-ray before you have even seen the specialist, since it is such a basic investigation in heart and chest disease.) Some X-rays, on the other hand, can only be performed on an appointments basis, and you may have to wait to have these done. Barium meals and enemas and IVPs (kidney X-rays) are examples of the sort of X-ray that you might have to wait for.

Apart from X-rays and blood tests there are many other tests that are carried out on an out-patient basis. Many of the patients passing through an out-patients department are likely to have an electrical recording of the heartbeat (ECG). Heart patients may also have ultrasound studies done on the heart, just as pregnant mothers attending the pre-natal clinic may have a routine ultrasound scan for their babies.

Just as ultrasound scans have added a great deal to the investigation of various problems, so have radioactive isotope scanning techniques. Radioactive isotopes are used for diagnosis and many big hospitals boast a large nuclear medicine department where these tests are carried out—here again many of them on out-patients.

Out-patient treatment
One of the largest hospital departments is likely to be the pharmacy, where all the drugs are dispensed for both the out-patients and the in-patients. Obviously the pharmacy of a big hospital will contain the widest possible range of drugs, and because it buys in bulk, it should obtain them from the drug companies at a cheaper rate than the ordinary drug store.

The pharmacy will only deal with drugs in the form of medicines, pills,

The emergency department is for accidents and emergencies. Changing a dressing is dealt within an out-patients department.

ointments etc. The specialists may also ask for all sorts of other medical items like surgical boots, surgical corsets, elastic stockings and so on, obtainable from the surgical appliance department.

Patients may also need other hospital services. One of the departments that has a large number of out-patients attending it is the physiotherapy department, where people requiring remedial treatment for all sorts of problems may attend. A patient there could have recently left his hospital bed after a stroke, for example, or he might have attended out-patients directly with a complaint like a frozen shoulder.

In the same way that you can have physiotherapy as an out-patient, you can also have speech therapy, osteopathy, hearing aids fitted and attention from the hospital social work department.

An increasing number of surgical procedures are also being carried out in out-patient departments. It has always been the case that minor operations, like the removal of sebaceous cysts or the freezing off of warts, were done under local anaesthetic as an out-patient. Many hospitals have an operating room in their out-patient departments for this purpose. There has also been an increase in the use of 'mini' D&Cs or 'vabra aspirations', in gynaecology out-patients, and surgeons now frequently carry out in their offices procedures like the injection of varicose veins, or hemorrhoids.

Radiotherapy (X-ray treatment, which is usually for cancer) can certainly be carried out on out-patients. The only difficulty with this is that the treatment itself can make people feel rather unwell, so that out-patient radiotherapy has to be reserved for those who are not badly affected by their underlying disease.

Since this treatment is often given every day, patients need to live within fairly easy reach of the hospital they attend.

One of the most striking growths in the business of out-patient care has been the recent innovation of 'day hospitals'. A big hospital might not only have a geriatric day hospital for the elderly, but also a psychiatric day hospital for those recovering from mental illness. These institutions provide a place for people in both the geriatric and the psychiatric groups who have difficulty in coping entirely by themselves in the community, but who are able to cope if they are given the support provided by a visit once, twice, or even five times a week to the day hospital. A day hospital may also be an appropriate place for active treatment in the form of physiotherapy.

The out-patient section of a hospital is now much more than a place where you go to be given pills by a physician, or to be advised to have an operation by a surgeon. There are very few things that cannot be done as an out-patient, and hospital admission is now reserved for those who really need it.

In larger hospitals, the pharmacy will be able to offer you a wider range of drugs than your local drugstore.

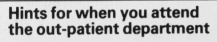

Hints for when you attend the out-patient department

● Do let the receptionist know when you arrive.
● Don't leave the waiting area without telling her.
● Do take a favorite toy or book if accompanying a young child.
● Don't plan anything too soon after your first visit, the doctor may send you off for tests which could take a long time.
● Do take all your medicines with you from home in the bottles they were in when you got them from the pharmacy.
● Do be prepared to pass a specimen of urine when you arrive—some hospitals ask you to bring one with you.
● Do expect to be examined all over on your first visit, whatever it is that you have wrong with you.
● Don't wear too many tight fitting clothes that are difficult to get on and take off.
● Do write down any questions that you want to ask the doctor.
● Don't be frightened to ask anything that you may want to know.
● Do take a relative or friend if you get confused or flustered.
● Do take an interpreter if your English is not very good.

P. Tweedie/Colorific!

Ovaries

Frank Kennard

Q My doctor tells me there is a chance that I may have to have one of my ovaries removed. Does this mean that I will be less fertile?

A No. What happens when one ovary is removed is that the other one grows slightly larger and takes over the work of its lost partner. Whereas with two ovaries you release eggs from them alternately, the single ovary will release one egg each month.

Q When do the ovaries first begin to work?

A A girl's ovaries may begin to release their first hormones as early as her seventh year. The effects of the hormones can be seen in a subtle change in her body shape, giving it a more womanly appearance. The changes are then followed by the start of breast development. It is likely that the sooner these changes begin, the earlier a girl will have her first menstrual period.

Q What happens to the ovaries when you are pregnant? Do they stop working?

A During pregnancy, the ovaries do stop releasing mature eggs. This results from the hormonal changes of pregnancy which suppress the output of hormones from the pituitary gland, the master gland that controls the production of hormones by the ovaries. In women who breast feed, the ovaries do not get back to normal until after the baby has been weaned, although eggs may be released sporadically during this time.

Q At what I think is the moment of ovulation, I sometimes get a dull pain in my tummy. What is this?

A This is what is known as Mittelschmerz (a German word for 'middle-pain'). The pain occurs when the egg is released. Not every woman experiences this, so it is not a reliable indicator of whether or not you are ovulating.

The ovaries not only produce and release eggs that are ready for fertilization. Their other vital role is to produce hormones that maintain the menstrual cycle and give a woman's body its feminine shape.

The ovaries are the parts of the female reproductive system which are designed to make and release mature ova or egg cells. When the ovum is fertilized by a sperm from a man it marks the start of a new human life. From the first period to the menopause, normal ovaries release one egg each month. They are also essential parts of the body's hormonal, or endocrine system.

Location and structure
The ovaries are two grey-pink, almond-shaped structures each about 3 cm (1.2 in) long and about 1 cm (0.4 in) thick. They are found in the pelvis, the body cavity bounded by the hip or pelvic bones, and lie one on each side of the uterus. Each ovary is held in place by strong, elastic ligaments. Just above each ovary is the feathery opening of the Fallopian tube

Site, structure and function of the ovaries

The ovaries are covered by a layer of cells. The cells which are destined to become eggs pass into the substance of the ovaries, where they are surrounded by a follicle membrane. Each month a single follicle matures, bursts on one ovary's surface and is released. If fertilized, the corpus luteum – which develops at the site of the egg's follicle – grows and secretes hormones that maintain pregnancy.

Fallopian tube

Ovary

Uterus

Primary follicles

Nutrient blood vessels

Corpus albicans (degenerated corpus luteum)

Ovum (egg)

Maturing follicle

Mature ovum (ovulation)

Mature corpus luteum

Developing corpus luteum

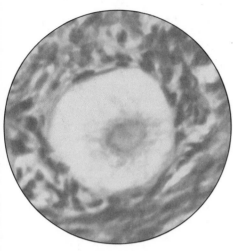

This histological (cell) slide is of a single ovum (egg). An egg is released each month from the ovary and enters the Fallopian tube where it may be fertilized.

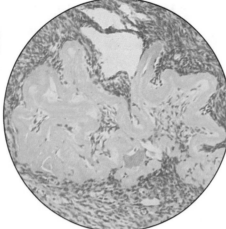

When no fertilization occurs, the corpus luteum, whose function it is to help sustain a pregnancy, withers into an irregular fibrous lump (corpus albicans).

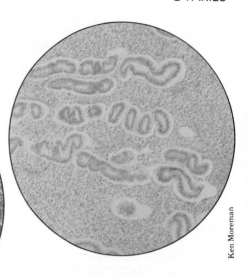

Ken Moreman

The endometrium, the lining of the uterus, which has been building up to allow implantation, is then shed during menstruation.

which leads to the womb, or uterus. Although they are very close to each other there is no direct connection between the ovary and the tube opening.

In a mature woman the ovaries have a rather lumpy appearance. The reason for this can be seen by looking at the internal structure under a microscope. Covering the ovary is a layer of cells called the germinal epithelium. It is from the cells in this border layer that the eggs or ova form; thousands of immature eggs, each in a round casing or follicle (the egg sac) can be seen clustered near the ovary edge.

Much more noticeable however are the follicles containing eggs in various stages of maturation. As these follicles enlarge, and after their eggs have been released, they produce the characteristic bumps on the ovary surface. The centre of the ovary is filled with elastic fibrous tissue which acts as a support for the follicle-containing outer layer.

Ovulation

Under a microscope, maturing follicles of the ovary can be seen as tiny balls enclosing a small mound of cells. In the centre of the mound is the egg cell in its final stages of maturation. When the follicle is ripe and the ovum mature, the cells at the follicle edge allow the ovum to leave. Exactly how this happens is still a mystery. The ovum is then wafted by the feathery ends, or fimbria, of the Fallopian tubes into the tube openings.

In their role as egg producers the ovaries also act as hormonal or endocrine glands. The ovaries function under the

control of the pituitary gland at the base of the brain. The pituitary first makes a hormone called follicle stimulating hormone (FSH) which travels in the bloodstream to the ovaries. FSH stimulates follicles and ovum development but it also brings about the secretion of the hormone oestrogen. Under oestrogen influence the lining of the uterus thickens in preparation for receiving a fertilized

egg. Oestrogen also stimulates the build up of body proteins and leads to fluid retention.

After a follicle has ripened and burst another pituitary hormone, luteinizing hormone, or LH, goes into action and brings about the development of the corpus luteum in the empty follicle. (The job of corpus luteum is to help establish a pregnancy). In turn, the corpus luteum

Though eggs are usually not released during breast feeding, it is not a reliable method of contraception, so take precautions.

Sandra Lausada

Q I read somewhere that at the time of ovulation, a woman feels much more sexy than usual. Is this really true?

A All women experience changes in their libido (sex drive). Some women feel most sexy at the time of ovulation, others during a period. This may even change from one month to the next.

Q Can you explain what happens to the ovaries and their eggs after the menopause?

A At the menopause, the ovaries stop making hormones and, as a result, they also stop releasing mature eggs. The many mature eggs remaining in the ovaries simply fail to develop any further. As the years after the menopause pass, the ovaries gradually shrink and become full of fibrous tissue which largely obliterates the remaining eggs.

Q Is it true that the contraceptive pill will interfere with the way the ovaries work?

A Yes. Because it contains artificial sex hormones, similar to the ones normally made by the ovaries, the Pill prevents eggs from maturing within the ovaries. The hormones of the Pill alter the body's natural monthly rhythm of hormone production, which in turn prevents the release of eggs. In effect, the body is tricked into thinking that it is pregnant, so that the ovaries get the message that they need not release any more eggs for the time being.

Q Is it possible to get an ovarian cyst after the change of life?

A Yes. Cysts can occur in a woman's ovaries up to the age of 60 and over, by which time the menopause or change of life will be over by many years. Ovarian cysts are growths which are usually harmless and are most common between the ages of 30 and 60. There is evidence that some cysts may arise as a result of the changing hormonal balance as the menopause approaches. They cause pain during intercourse and a swelling of the lower abdomen, sometimes to a great degree so that a woman appears to be pregnant.

makes and releases its own hormone, progesterone. If the egg is not fertilized within a fortnight the corpus luteum shrinks, progesterone production is turned off, and the lining of the uterus is shed as the monthly menstrual period (see Menstruation, pp 1169-73). Now FSH production begins again and the whole cycle is repeated. If, however, the egg has been fertilized (see Conception, pp 309-10), then the corpus luteum goes on working until the placenta is established and there is no bleeding.

Ovary development
Ovary development is largely complete by the time the female foetus is in the third month of life in the womb, and few major changes will take place until puberty. By the time a baby girl is born her ovaries contain, between them, from 40,000 to 300,000 primary follicles, each containing an immature egg. At most only 500 or so of these eggs will ever be released, and probably no more than half a dozen—if that—will develop into new human beings.

When the ovaries first start to make the hormone oestrogen, they are not yet capable of releasing mature eggs. These early oestrogens bring about the physical changes of puberty (see Menarche, pp 1160-61) such as growth of breasts, widening of hips and pubic hair. These changes begin at least a year before a girl

has her first period, and are a sign that the oestrogens have begun to stimulate the release of mature eggs.

What can go wrong
Apart from the normal failure of the ovaries at menopause (see pp 1166-8), the most common problem of the ovaries is the formation of ovarian cysts. These growths, which are usually benign, may grow to such vast proportions that they make a woman's abdomen swell up as if she were pregnant. Many small ovarian cysts often disappear of their own accord and cysts usually cause pain only when they become twisted within the ovary (see Cyst, pp 341-2).

Examining the ovaries
From the outside of the body, the only way a doctor can examine the ovaries is by feeling, or palpating them (see Internal examination, pp 865-6).

For a more thorough internal examination a technique called laparoscopy is used. Under a general anaesthetic, carbon dioxide gas is injected into the pelvic cavity. This makes the intestines move away from their normal position, so that they no longer obscure the ovaries. A tubular instrument, the laparoscope, is inserted through or near the navel. The surgeon can then look directly at the ovaries and if he wishes take a tissue sample or biopsy.

Ovarian cysts

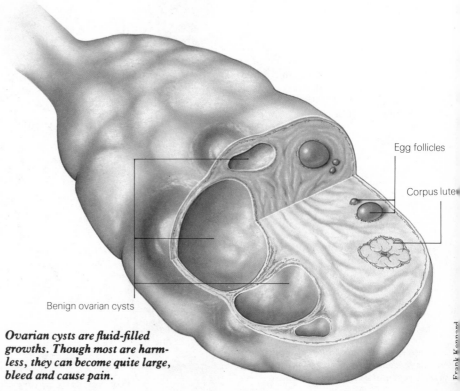

Egg follicles

Corpus luteum

Benign ovarian cysts

Ovarian cysts are fluid-filled growths. Though most are harmless, they can become quite large, bleed and cause pain.

Frank Kennard

Overbreathing

Q I feel sluggish when I get up in the mornings. Is it a good idea to have several good deep breaths at an open window?

A Fully expanding the lungs with fresh air is a good way of getting rid of lethargy. But don't overdo the deep breaths or you might feel peculiar, lightheaded and ill.

Q Is it possible that my teenage son may be able to fake overbreathing to stay off school?

A You must try and discover whether he is deliberately overbreathing or whether it is happening because he is worrying about school. If he is genuinely anxious about going to school, have a chat with his teacher and talk to him yourself about his problems. If you think he is deliberately overbreathing, make it clear that you are not going to be manipulated and send him to school.

Q I have been told that the funny turns I have been having are caused by overbreathing, but how can the doctor be sure?

A Although it seems very difficult to be sure, there are often very strong clues that hyperventilation is the underlying problem. One test is to ask a patient to overbreathe deliberately and see if this produces the symptoms. There is an even more definite sign though, and this is called Chvostek's sign. When people have dropped the level of carbon dioxide in their blood because of overbreathing, some of their nerves become rather irritable. This can be demonstrated by tapping the nerve that supplies the muscles of the face just as it emerges from inside the skull at the bottom of the ear. A light tap of the finger produces a twitch in the corner of the mouth, a sign that only occurs in overbreathing, or where there is a low level of calcium.

Q My grandmother sometimes has panting fits. Is this overbreathing?

A No. Overbreathing is very rare in the elderly, and panting or shortness of breath should be investigated by a doctor.

Overbreathing is generally caused by stress and it can produce some very worrying symptoms.

Because breathing is something that happens automatically in the body, we all take it for granted. But as soon as we become aware of air passing into and out of our lungs, we can then choose to breathe more frequently and more deeply if we wish. If this overbreathing is done for a few minutes or more, we will experience peculiar feelings. This condition is also known as hyperventilation.

Overbreathing often occurs in stressful situations. Patients might go to their doctors with a variety of symptoms, and it can prove very difficult for the doctor to diagnose overbreathing as the cause. It is a rare condition in the very young and elderly and is most commonly seen in young women between 15 and 30 years.

Causes
An adult normally breathes in and out about 15-20 times a minute when he or she is resting—this rate will increase naturally under stressful conditions and with some lung disorders. However, some people hyperventilate with stress and experience strange symptoms which can be very worrying.

Overdosage with aspirin also causes hyperventilation because of the direct action of the drug on the centre in the brain which controls breathing rates.

Symptoms
The symptoms caused by hyperventilation are the result of breathing out too much carbon dioxide gas. Increased breathing reduces the carbon dioxide in

Overbreathing in teenage girls can be easily cured by getting them to breathe for a few minutes into a paper bag.

the tissues, causing narrowing of the blood vessels in the brain and reducing the blood flow.

Faintness, visual disturbances, nausea, cramps, unsteadiness, headache, shortness of breath, palpitations, hot flushes, cold sweats and tingling sensations are the symptoms experienced.

Treatment
The quickest way to cure overbreathing is to breathe in and out of a paper bag, taking in the air and carbon dioxide that has just been breathed out. This increases the carbon dioxide level in the blood and the symptoms disappear. Mild tranquillizers may also help to control anxiety.

Outlook
Many people 'grow out' of these attacks, but for a few, long-term psychiatric treatment is necessary. Avoiding stressful situations does help. Tranquillizers may be prescribed if the condition is severe but taking them for a long time should be avoided.

Ron Sutherland

Overcrowding

Q My father has died and I'd like to have my mother to live with us. The problem is that we have a full house already and my husband says we shall be overcrowded if she stays with us. He says she should take up the offer of a flat in a senior citizen complex near the centre of town. This seems hard-hearted to me. Who is right?

A Your husband. The strain that overcrowding would cause would make both you and your mother unhappy, and it would not solve the problem. You'll probably find that your mother, like most old people, prefers living with people of her own age, and near the convenience of the shops. You can visit her regularly and show her your love that way.

Q I know a couple who are being treated by the doctor for illnesses that he says may be related to their housing conditions. Since they live alone in a two bedroomed 15th floor flat, this seems like nonsense. Is he wrong?

A No. The problems and illnesses caused by overcrowding are very similar to those experienced in a high-rise flat. The proximity of neighbours and the noise they make, worrying about the noise that you yourself make, the feeling of being hemmed in: these factors can be regarded as overcrowding and can lead to illness.

Q I live on my own and never speak to a soul from one end of the week to the other. It makes me mad to hear people complain about overcrowding – don't they know it's nicer to have company than to be like me?

A It's not just a question of having company – people who live in overcrowded conditions have no space for themselves or time alone. But your problem of isolation can be as bad if you let it—the mental problems caused by isolation are similar to those caused by overcrowding. Try to get out: find out about clubs in your area – your doctor may know of some that are suitable.

When people live in overcrowded conditions they suffer in many ways: not only are they likely victims of a rising crime rate, vandalism and all forms of violence, but their general health can also be affected.

Jonathan T. Wright/Bruce Coleman Ltd

As the population of the world increases by many thousands each day, we all need to be aware of the problems that can be caused by overcrowding. For instance, it can be a cause of certain social problems—a rising crime rate, vandalism and all forms of violence. It can give rise to personal problems that may result in mental disorders, or cause people to commit suicide, and it can lead to health problems—particularly among children—including the spread of diseases and a higher death rate.

Just a glance at the statistics will show that delinquency rates are highest amongst those who live in the centre of a city, and overcrowding is probably a key factor. The figures gradually decrease in the less crowded surrounding surburbs.

The hustle and bustle of life in a crowded city may appeal to some, but it can result in serious problems for many inhabitants.

The number of mental hospital admissions can also be related to some extent to living conditions.

Overcrowding is a term that is not only used to describe the number of people occupying a household or a room, but also the number of people living in any given area. It is thus possible to understand why people living in a high-rise block of flats may have similar problems to those who live too many to a room.

Living too close
When animals are experimentally placed in conditions that are far more over-

1456

crowded than normal they start to behave very oddly. One of their instincts seems to be to curb the growth in population and they resort to sexual relations with their own sex. They congregate around communal areas such as food troughs and develop very aggressive behaviour towards each other.

The policy of building large blocks of flats to house families brought with it a number of unforeseen social problems.

Human beings, too, react differently from normal when they live in overcrowded conditions. Sometimes physical proximity can induce comradeship, but it is more likely to be the cause of conflict and strife. It has been found that people tend to compensate for excessive physical proximity by creating an emotional distance around themselves as a substitute for privacy. This is why, in some larger families where the children sleep several to a bed, as they get older the siblings react by having less contact with each other than those from smaller families.

Overcrowding and health

As no one would choose to live in badly overcrowded conditions if they could afford a spacious alternative, it is clear that overcrowding often goes hand in hand with poverty. This can mean a number of related problems. There may be a lack of hot water and facilities for cleaning. Food storage may be inadequate, and there may be only an outside toilet. These factors may make it difficult to maintain high standards of hygiene. Physical proximity also means that communicable diseases can spread through overcrowded dwellings at great speed.

Children tend to suffer most in such conditions: they may get the childhood illnesses at an earlier age, and often more severely, resulting in permanent disability or infant death.

Some illnesses can be found more often in overcrowded conditions than elsewhere. Sometimes this is the result of the physical closeness, at other times the result of the poverty. Among these are:

Tuberculosis: one of the most important factors in the spread of tuberculosis is overcrowding. It is spread by infected sputum and coughing. When it is impossible to isolate the sufferer, it is clear that others will risk getting the illness.

Digestive diseases: some of these are related to poor food and insanitary food storage, as well as poor toilet facilities.

Pneumonia: this inflammation of the lungs can be fatal to both children and old people.

Otitis media: this is inflammation of the middle ear.

Meningitis: this illness is an inflammation of the membranes surrounding the brain and the spinal cord. The virus that causes meningitis often takes hold if the person is subject to damp, cold and overcrowding.

Infectious skin diseases, acute dyspepsia and anaemia are other illnesses also associated with people who live in overcrowded conditions.

There is also a great risk from accidents in the home, with fire being the greatest hazard of all. These can affect all age groups.

The rise in violence and crime

It is obvious that crime of all sorts – vandalism, robbery, rape, and violence –

Q Will my three-year-old son suffer from being brought up in a high-rise flat?

A Some young children find it difficult living high up. On ground level it would be easier for him to go out to play while you kept an eye on him. He needs space to be able to run around. You should try to take him to a playground at least once a day – or best of all, send him to a playgroup. Take him to parks at weekends so that he can let off some steam.

Q There are more people living in our house than in any other in the street. We like it that way, but I think that the neighbours talk about it, which makes me feel embarrassed. Are we overcrowded?

A No you are not. If you are happy the way you are, then it is completely unimportant what the neighbours think. They may envy your friendly set-up.

Q They say that a major cause of tuberculosis is overcrowding – but isn't tuberculosis an illness of the past?

A No, it's still around, but the number of cases is only a fraction of what it was a few generations ago. In addition, the treatment available has cut the death rate from the illness right down.

Q Some people like to live close together. How do you define overcrowding?

A There are no specific numbers after which a place is automatically considered overcrowded. It mainly depends on how the inhabitants experience the conditions. In some densely populated cities, such as Hong Kong, people expect to live in more or less squashed conditions; this means that the level of crowding at which people show unhealthy physical or mental symptoms is much higher than it is elsewhere. However, someone who moves from a rural village to a town may feel claustrophobic in conditions that do not seem crowded to the town dweller.

Overcrowding and social problems

Less than one person per room

More than one person per room

More than one and a half people per room

More than two people per room

More than two and a half people per room

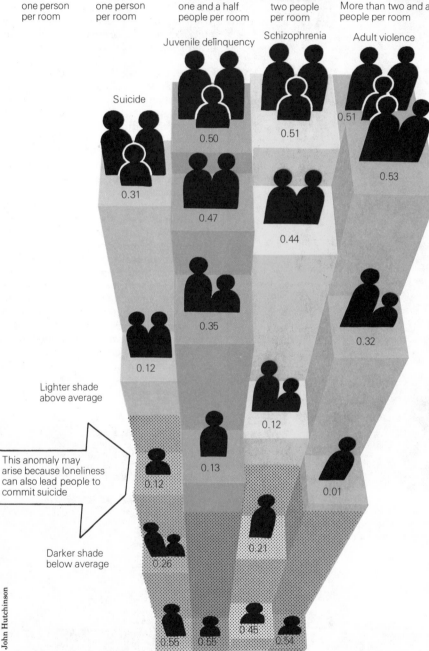

Suicide — 0.31 — 0.12 — 0.12 — 0.26 — 0.55

Juvenile delinquency — 0.50 — 0.47 — 0.35 — 0.13 — 0.55

Schizophrenia — 0.51 — 0.44 — 0.12 — 0.21 — 0.45

Adult violence — 0.51 — 0.53 — 0.32 — 0.01 — 0.54

Lighter shade above average

This anomaly may arise because loneliness can also lead people to commit suicide

Darker shade below average

John Hutchinson

This graph relates the number of people living per room to four different social problems. The statistics come from a survey done in the late 1970s. The point at which the darker and lighter shades meet on the graph represents the average number of, for example, suicides per thousand people. If the average is, say, 2.0 suicides per thousand population, then for people living more than one but less than one-and-a-half persons per room this figure is reduced by 0.55 to a rate of 1.45 suicides per thousand. The pattern linking these problems with overcrowding is clear.

is more common in inner city and overcrowded areas. Other factors contribute to this, though, such as unemployment, racial tension and lack of money. So how important is the overcrowding factor? A comprehensive study in America carried out over three years, looked at just this question.

The study involved two groups of 300 families who were chosen because they were similar in most respects: they all earned very little, and roughly corresponded in age of father, mother and children and in the size of the families. But one group lived in overcrowded slums while the other group had recently moved to a special housing scheme.

The most dramatic difference that emerged between the two groups during the study was in health. The children and adults on the housing scheme were much healthier than the other group. But there were other interesting differences too. Neighbours got on better with each other on the housing scheme and made strong and lasting friendships: this developed into a feeling of community that was conspicuously lacking in the other group. There were fewer feuds and conflicts between families and fewer fights.

Other differences between the two groups also emerged. Social standing improved in the families of the housing scheme and the children were doing better at school. They saw themselves as people who would break out of the low income bracket and go on to achieve more than their parents.

High-rise living

If you live hemmed in by other people above, below and to either side of you, then you are living in overcrowded conditions – even if there is enough space in your flat for all of you. The loss of privacy caused by living in such close proximity to neighbours that you are affected by their noise, cooking smells, and other indications of their nearness can result in many problems of tension. This may be compounded by the fact that you may well worry about how you are inconveniencing your neighbours – by your noise, and so on. Most illnesses that result from high-rise living are of a kind arising from tension. These may include hypertension, neurosis, and anti-social behaviour.

A stark contrast in urban environments: a crowded street in New York's Lower East Side (above) and an open, leafy green in Sydney, Australia.

Children are most likely to be badly affected by life in a high-rise flat—both on their own account, and also because they are likely to absorb the discontentment of their mothers.

Children between the ages of three and six suffer most. This is the age when they really need to use up surplus energy running around and playing out of doors. The higher up they live, the less time they are likely to spend outside. Confinement in the home causes two major problems. Their physical movement has to be restricted and shouting is forbidden because of the neighbours.

Overdoses

Q If I take a couple of aspirins for a headache and they have no effect, how long should I wait before taking any more?

A Most medicines are intended to be taken three or four times a day, with usually four hours as the shortest safe interval between doses. This applies to aspirin and so it would be safe to take another two in four hours. If your headache was really persistent, you could make it every three hours.

If the headache is still giving trouble in two days' time you must go to a doctor, rather than just take more aspirin.

Q How safe is it to take medicines, bought over the counter, as often as you like?

A Not at all safe. The fact that some medicines are available without a doctor's prescription does not mean that there is no risk attached to misusing them. It is vital to follow the manufacturer's instructions for taking even the mildest drugs.

Q I have been taking iron tablets for a year. Isn't there a danger of their effect building up to an overdose?

A No, because the body excretes what it cannot absorb. The excess passes out of the body in the urine and the faeces. An overdose can occur, however, if a substance is given in sufficiently massive amounts to do immediate harm.

Q If I were accidentally to give my one-year-old too much junior aspirin how would I know that he had been given an overdose?

A If you had given him only one tablet too many, there would probably be no unusual signs.

But this is not to say that you must not be extremely careful giving medicines to children: their small body size makes them that much more vulnerable to overdose.

The usual symptom of aspirin overdose is undue drowsiness, or difficulty in waking the patient.

Many people think of an overdose purely in terms of attempted suicide, but accidents with drugs are every bit as common as deliberate misuse.

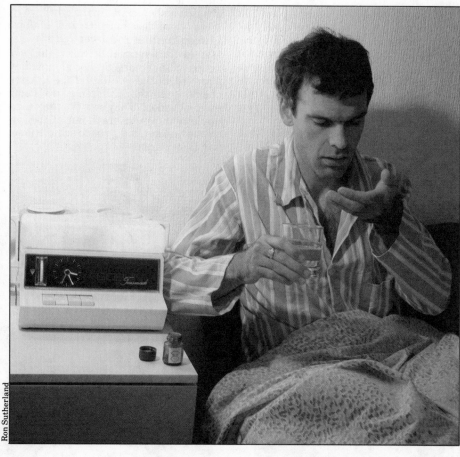

Ron Sutherland

Overdose has become a subject of major concern among doctors, and it is one which everyone should know about because almost always a tragedy can be avoided by following a few simple rules about when and how to take medicines.

Very occasionally, overdose happens because a doctor or a chemist makes a mistake in prescribing, making up or labelling a drug; but the majority of cases arise out of the user's carelessness.

Care should be taken with all drugs, not just the ones that are obviously potent. Everyday medicines like aspirin are killers if taken in sufficient quantities, and so are many chemicals found around the house.

Children and overdose

Children are the commonest victims of accidental overdose. They are much more gravely affected by drugs than adults, partly because of their small body size and partly because drugs intended for adults are exactly that: they can harm a

Carelessness about the number and mixture of drugs taken can end in an overdose. A typical overdose situation may begin by taking another sleeping pill during the night because the first dose didn't seem to work. The next morning a few painkillers are needed for a toothache, and tranquillizers are taken to calm the nerves after a row at breakfast. More stress at work means more tranquillizers, followed by a liquid lunch. The possible result from all this pill-taking, combined with alcohol: collapse from an accidental overdose.

child even if a tiny amount is given. Most medicines for children are specially prepared as such, made up so that they can be given in 5 ml (one teaspoonful) doses. Children should not be given medicines other than those specifically meant for them.

It is possible for medicines taken by a pregnant woman to pass to the foetus in sufficient quantities to affect it. So no medicines should be taken during a

pregnancy without first consulting a doctor for advice.

Drugs can also be passed from a mother to her baby while breast feeding. Again, the simple and necessary precaution is to consult a doctor.

Most overdoses among children occur, however, because children get hold of and swallow their parents' medicines out of curiosity. It is common sense to store medicines where children cannot get at them. Remember that children can always climb or scramble or crawl further than you think is possible.

Many tablets look, to children, like sweets, so to stop them making such potentially fatal comparisons, do not let them see you taking pills. Another good reason for taking medicines discreetly is that young children love to copy grown-ups. If it is good for mummy and daddy, it must, they think, be good for them too.

Adults and overdose

Forgetting whether or not you have had a particular tablet, or medicine, and taking another just to be sure, is the greatest risk. If this happens two or three times a day, or just once with a potent drug, overdose may occur.

Taking another dose 'just to be sure' is especially likely when the patient has to take several different drugs each day. To avoid mistakes, put the whole of the day's tablets out in a small container—for example an egg cup—checking each time, with a careful read of the label, that the drugs really are what you think they are.

Also check the instructions, however familiar you think you may be with them. Doctors and nurses do this every time they give a patient medicine; so why should you be less careful?

Never take tablets or medicine from a bottle that is without a label, or where the label has become illegible, even if you are sure you can recognize what is inside. There are now many thousands of drugs available and not enough combinations of colour, size and shape for them all to look different so mistakes can be made.

Q I am terrified that my four-year-old son will accidentally take one of my contraceptive pills. What would happen if he did?

A Probably not much, but there is the danger that he will eat the whole lot, and this might cause vomiting. So if you think a child has swallowed drugs of this or any other sort, you should take him to a hospital for a check-up.

More to the point, why do you leave tablets about where your son can get hold of them? Take more care to hide them, and you'll have no need to be terrified.

Q What do I do if I find a member of my family has overdosed? I've heard some people say you should make them sick, while others tell you it's dangerous to do that. What's the best thing to do?

A The first thing you should do is call an ambulance: prompt hospital treatment is vital in all cases of overdose.

Whether or not you should make the patient sick depends on how long it is since the patient took the overdose, and whether or not they are unconscious.

If the patient is unconscious, on no account attempt to induce vomiting. The overdose will have already entered the system, and when someone is senseless there is a danger that vomit will get into the lungs and cause death by 'drowning'.

However, if you are confronted by someone who tells you they have just—say within the last half hour—swallowed a bottle of sleeping pills, you could save their life by making them vomit.

The method is to stick two fingers—index and middle—right down the hole at the back of the throat as far you can reach. Hold the mouth open with the other hand—if you don't, you may get bitten. Do not, under any circumstances, induce vomiting by giving the patient salt water to drink. Although this used to be the recommended course of action, it is often ineffective and can be dangerous.

Wait for the ambulance. When it comes, give the crew the bottle of whatever drug has been taken – even if it is empty. This is usually vital for diagnostic purposes in hospital.

Safety with drugs

Ron Sutherland

● Keep all medicines in a lockable, dark cupboard out of the reach of children. Use child-proof containers. Don't let children handle medicines, or see you taking them.

● Do not keep medicines longer than a year. In any case don't keep them longer than their expiry date. Destroy completely what is left of a medicine after you have finished it, but don't throw it in the wastebasket, or onto a fire.

● If a doctor has prescribed a medicine, complete the course. If in doubt, ask a doctor or a pharmacist.

● Tell your doctor of any side-effect experienced from a medicine.

● If you are advised not to drink, drive or operate machinery while taking a medicine, don't: it can be dangerous.

● Always read the directions on the label; always take exactly the recommended dose.

● Never treat any problem yourself for longer than a week without consulting your doctor.

● If a medicine you have used according to the instructions fails to have the right effect, consult your doctor.

● Only give young children medicines which are described on the package as suitable for them.

● Do not take any medicine during pregnancy, or while breast feeding, without the advice of a doctor.

● If you are being treated by one doctor, do not, without consulting him, take any medicine prescribed for you by another doctor; indeed don't take *any* other medicine without telling your doctor as the drugs could interact.

Even doctors and nurses can sometimes be in doubt about the identity of a tablet or capsule, and have to refer to a complicated table; so again, why be less careful yourself?

Doubting the medicine

Sometimes a medicine does not have the expected or desired effect, and the patient starts to doubt it. This is potentially dangerous, too, because the temptation arises to increase the dose slightly, or take it at shorter intervals.

This may seem an obvious error, but it happens surprisingly often, sometimes with tragic results. Another temptation, especially strong for those who are already unwell and cannot spare the time to get to the doctor, is to take medicine which has been prescribed for someone else in the household on the assumption that it sounds as if it might help. This, too, can be fatal.

Similarly, it is unwise to take additional medicines, even ones bought over the counter at a drugstore, while you are already on a course of drugs. They can combine with each other so there is a clash, or they can potentiate each other—exaggerating each other's effects. So consult your doctor before taking *any* drug while already on another.

Symptoms of overdose

These vary, of course, according to the drug involved and the amount taken. However, indications of mild overdose, (which should still be reported to a doctor) include dizziness, faintness, blurring of the vision, drowsiness, difficulty in concentration and a mild degree of mental confusion. Perhaps there will be some disorientation—overdose victims may not know where they are or exactly how they came to be there.

More serious overdose is characterized by falling about, being difficult to arouse from a deep sleep and slipping into full unconsciousness.

Outlook

Obviously it is worth knowing the relevant first aid procedures for overdose. Provided they are followed promptly, the outlook for the patient is good. Inevitably the hospital plays the major role in treatment, and here there are three things doctors can do: resuscitation in the intensive care unit, stomach washing and chemical antidotes.

Provided treatment is early enough, the patient almost always recovers, with no after-effects. But the most important point about overdoses is that prevention makes so much more sense than cure.

Oxygen

Q How can you tell if someone is short of oxygen?

A If a patient has blueness around the lips you can assume that the level of oxygen in his blood is lower than it should be.

Q My husband is in hospital and is being given oxygen. Does this mean that he will always need this extra supply?

A No, he is most unlikely to need additional oxygen when he comes out of hospital. The usual reason why people are given oxygen in hospital is because they have an acute heart problem, or infection in the chest when they already suffer from a long-term chest ailment. The extra oxygen is necessary only to tide them over the immediate difficulty, and it is controlled very carefully.

Q What is an oxygen debt?

A If you walk or run a long distance, your muscles use most of the oxygen in the bloodstream and your heart and lungs work hard to keep the level as high as possible. All in all, however, the system remains in balance. But if you do something that requires a lot of energy over a short time—like running fast for 200 metres—your muscles use up more oxygen than the heart can immediately provide. The muscles can do this because they draw on an oxygen store in the form of a compound called myoglobin. Once the stored oxygen is used up it has to be replaced, and this is called an oxygen debt.

Q I often feel very tired and lethargic. Is this because I am running short of oxygen?

A No, almost certainly not. Everybody feels tired from time to time but oxygen lack is hardly ever the reason. Some heart or lung conditions can make you short of oxygen so that you get breathless with any sort of exercise. Anaemia, however, can cause a person to become tired and listless, and it does involve a low oxygen level. Consult your doctor if you think you may be anaemic.

We cannot live for more than a few minutes if our supply of oxygen is cut off. It is the single most important substance on which our lives depend.

Oxygen makes up about a fifth of the air that we breathe, and the work of the lungs, the heart and the blood vessels is primarily concerned with carrying oxygen from the air to the body's tissues, where it is needed to produce the energy that they require in order to stay alive.

Oxygen is an odourless, tasteless and colourless gas. Its main source on Earth is from living green plants.

What oxygen does

Oxygen is essential for the production of energy. Just as a car burns petrol with oxygen, and a coal fire uses both coal and the oxygen in a room to produce heat, so the body's cells use oxygen in exactly the same way: they burn up their fuel – which usually comes in the form of sugar – with oxygen to produce energy. The waste products of this chemical reaction are the same in both the body's cells and the car – namely carbon dioxide and water. Although some of the body's cells are able to function for a while without oxygen, the brain cannot.

Oxygen from the air is inhaled, then absorbed by the lungs and carried in the blood to the body tissues. When the amount of oxygen needed for a particular physical task is greater than can be supplied at the time, an 'oxygen debt' results. A person makes up the supply by panting and breathing deeply so as to take in as much oxygen as possible immediately after the period of exertion.

Oxygen deficiency

There are two main groups of people likely to suffer from a shortage of oxygen

Oxygen masks can be uncomfortable – 'nasal spectacles', tubes which go into each nostril, are much less daunting.

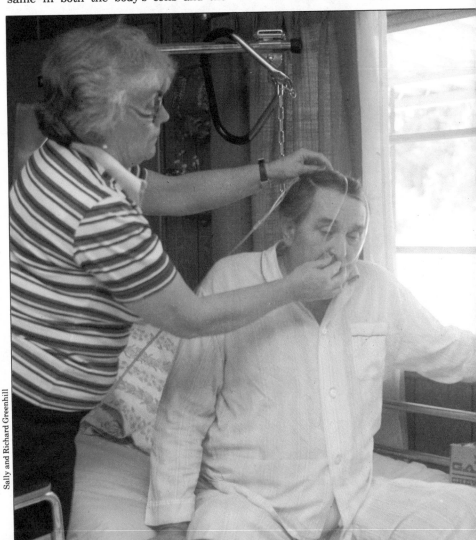

Sally and Richard Greenhill

in the blood: those with lung disease, and those with the sort of heart complaint that keeps the lungs short of blood.

A lack of oxygen shows up as a blueness around the lips and tongue, which is known medically as cyanosis. Haemoglobin, the red pigment in blood which takes up oxygen in the lungs, carries it to the tissues where it is released. Saturated haemoglobin is haemoglobin that has its full amount of oxygen; it then is red in colour. But haemoglobin with insufficient oxygen tends to be more purple. Hence a preponderance of low-oxygen haemo-

The path oxygen takes through the body

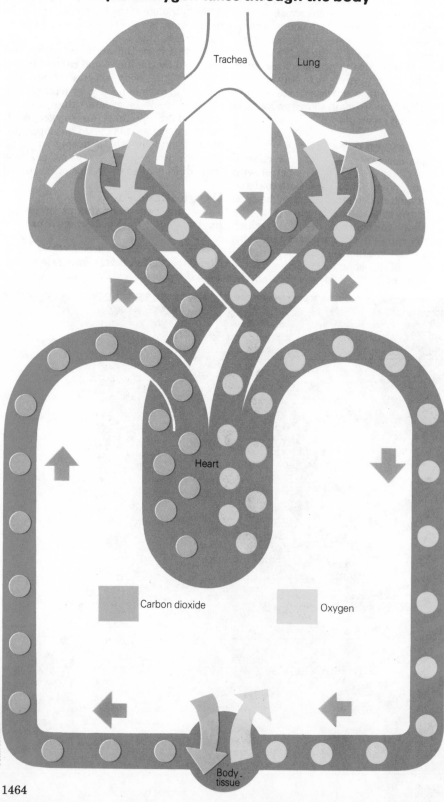

Trachea
Lung
Heart
Carbon dioxide
Oxygen
Body tissue

John Hutchinson

1464

Ron Sutherland

globin leads to the blue look of cyanosis.

Almost any sort of lung condition can lead to a low level of oxygen in the blood. Chronic bronchitis is perhaps the most common. It is often combined with emphysema, a disease in which the lung tissue is destroyed to such an extent that fewer air-sacs than normal are available for the exchange of oxygen between blood and tissues.

A lack of oxygen is also associated with acute attacks of asthma. It is often found during severe spasms among asthmatics who also get chronic bronchitis. Pneumonia, too, may also lead to cyanosis. And it may be necessary to give oxygen to people who have suffered a heart attack, as the flow of blood – and hence the delivery of oxygen to the body's tissues – will have been drastically reduced.

Giving extra oxygen

An oxygen mask is the commonest way for oxygen to be given. The type of mask used in hospitals allows doctors to regulate the percentage of oxygen in the air that the patient breathes. The aim is to raise the level of oxygen in the blood until it reaches normal. The level of oxygen in the blood can be monitored by

Oxygen from the lungs is pumped around the body by the heart. The cells of body tissue exchange it for carbon dioxide which is finally exhaled.

– for a prolonged period will succumb to a form of pneumonia. A more common problem, however, is encountered with those patients who have suffered from respiratory failure.

This is a condition in which lung disease causes abnormalities in the way the brain controls breathing. Breathing becomes laboured when the level of oxygen in the blood becomes low. At the same time the proportion of carbon dioxide increases.

Normally, the rising level of carbon dioxide prompts the brain to devote more work to respiration. But in someone who suffers from respiratory failure, it is the level of oxygen that determines the brain's response. If a patient with respiratory failure is given extra oxygen he will in effect be encouraged to breathe in *less* air, so making matters worse. The level of carbon dioxide will then rise and may eventually lead to unconsciousness. Levels of oxygen given to patients are always very carefully controlled.

Sea air is thought to be especially invigorating. It contains a higher proportion of ozone—a form of oxygen made up of three atoms rather than two.

taking samples of arterial blood.

Some people find a mask uncomfortable so they may be given oxygen through what are called 'nasal spectacles'. These are simply tubes, one placed under each nostril, through which the extra oxygen can be inhaled.

Babies and small children may be put inside an 'oxygen tent'. If the baby is premature, the oxygen may be fed directly into its incubator. Very great care is needed in the amount of oxygen given to premature babies, as too high a level can lead to a disease that may cause blindness.

In all cases the oxygen will either be piped from a central supply within the hospital, or individual cylinders of oxygen will be used.

Low levels of oxygen in the body's tissues may be treated by putting the patient into a small room where the oxygen is more concentrated than usual and also supplied at a higher than normal pressure. It is known as hyperbaric (high-pressure) oxygen. This treatment has a small but valuable place in modern medicine. It is used to treat carbon monoxide poisoning, when people are distressed from inhaling acrid smoke, and in cases of gas gangrene (see Gangrene, page 549).

Too much of a good thing

Anyone who breathes a very high concentration of oxygen – more than 60 per cent

Jessical Ehiers/Bruce Coleman Ltd

The oxygen cycle

Green plants are the main source of oxygen for all animals, including man. In plants a chemical reaction called photosynthesis, which is set off by sunlight, takes place when carbon dioxide and water absorbed by the plant form starch in the leaves and also give off oxygen. The oxygen is breathed in by animals and, in return, carbon dioxide is exhaled and used by plants, thus forming a continuous cycle of interdependence.

In addition animals, including man, eat plant leaves and the starch is broken down into sugars which, when acted upon by oxygen, release energy.

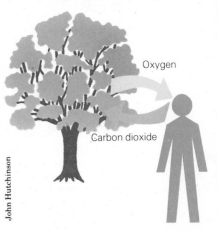

Oxygen

Carbon dioxide

John Hutchinson

Pacemaker

Q My mother is going to have a pacemaker put in. Will there be a large bump on the skin?

A Modern pacing boxes are about the size of a matchbox, and although this is fairly small, in most patients a bump is inescapable. Pacing boxes are usually fitted on the front of the chest, about two inches below the middle of the collar-bone. If your mother is of average weight, most of the bump may well be lost in the breast tissue.

Q If my pacemaker packs up, will my heart stop beating?

A Only a minority of patients with pacemakers are so dependent on them that their hearts would stop completely if their pacemaker ceased working. Most patients would simply have the symptoms of very slow pulse rate – dizziness or blackouts, or lethargy on exertion. The object of the design of pacemakers is to prevent sudden pacemaker failure occurring. There is, however, a tiny risk of pacing box failure if there is a sudden shift of the pacing wire: this sometimes occurs soon after the pacing system has been put in, if at all.

You should be attending a pacemaker clinic regularly and they will check the electrical function of your unit. Eventually batteries run down, but the clinic will have plenty of warning about this. It is a relatively simple operation to replace the pacing box.

Q If I needed a pacemaker in an emergency, how quickly could it be put in?

A Many doctors have enough experience of the technique to put a temporary pacing wire into the heart without X-rays to help them, in which case it could be a matter of two or three minutes to get some sort of pacing activity. In a real emergency, it is possible to get a heart working again by passing a wire directly into it through the chest wall by means of a long needle. Usually, though, there is time to get the patient to X-ray facilities. Remember patients can be kept alive for hours by using external heart massage.

One of the most dramatic advances in medical technology has been the development of pacemakers for the heart – saving many patients from death or disablement.

We rely on the regular beating of our hearts to stay alive. This regular heartbeat depends upon the heart's own natural pacemaker – the part of the heart called the sino-atrial node. The sino-atrial node initiates impulses that then spread through the heart via a system of specialized electrical conducting tissues. The entire electrical timing system is called the conducting system of the heart (see pp 655-6).

Who needs a pacemaker
Unfortunately, the heart's own pacing system can sometimes go wrong. This can occur as a result of ischaemic heart disease, a hardening or blocking of the coronary arteries. Alternatively, a heart attack may give rise to conducting system difficulties, requiring that a pacemaker be put in as a matter of urgency. Often these pacemakers are only temporary as the heart may recover its ability to control its own timing. If and when this occurs, the pacemaker will be removed.

The majority of patients who require a permanent pacemaker are those in whom the conducting system has broken down entirely. There is no obvious cause for this—it is almost as though the conducting system has worn out. The condition is more common in the elderly. In fact, most patients who need pacemakers are over the age of 65.

When the heart stops conducting electrical impulses properly, the heart rate slows down; this is known as heart block or arrhythmia. The condition may be variable, leading to sudden attacks of fainting and unconsciousness. The heart may even stop completely, and if emergency treatment isn't given, death will result. On the other hand, patients may suffer from a continuously slow pulse rate. Although this is satisfactory to keep patients well while they're resting, it leads to lethargy and breathlessness upon exertion, which is severely disabling.

How a pacemaker works
The basic principle in all the various sorts of pacemaker is exactly the same. Two parts make up the pacing system. First there is some electronic means of producing regular electrical impulses that are of the correct strength and duration to cause the ventricles, the main pumping chambers of the heart, to beat. This impulse is conducted to the heart by a wire, called a pacing lead, whose tip is implanted somewhere in the substance of the ventricles. Provided the impulses are strong enough, and there is good electrical connection between the wire and the muscle of the ventricle, a heartbeat will result from each impulse.

To co-ordinate the timing of the heartbeat, an impulse generator, or pacing box, sends electrical impulses to the heart via the pacing wire. This enables it to 'know' when there has been a heartbeat so that it doesn't send another impulse until the heart is ready. This is called demand pacing, and is almost always the system used as it allows the heart specialist to programme the pacemaker.

What happens then is that the pacing box is set at a given rate, say 60 beats per minute. This means that the box will produce an impulse every second, unless it senses that the heart has produced a beat on its own. If the heart does do this, the pacing box will then wait for another second before producing its next impulse, and so on.

This chest X-ray shows the two main components of a pacemaker in place: the pacing box and the lead to the heart.

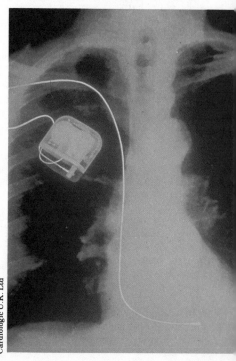

Cardiologic U.K. Ltd

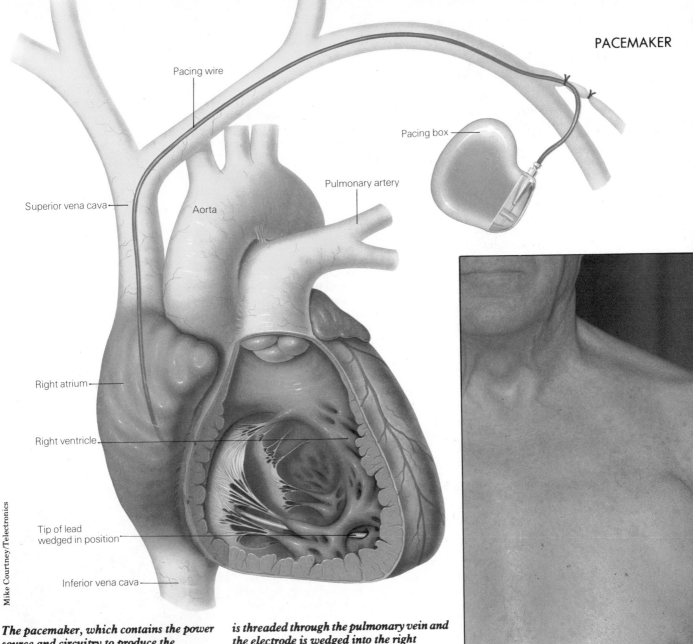

Pacing wire

Pacing box

Pulmonary artery

Aorta

Superior vena cava

Right atrium

Right ventricle

Tip of lead
wedged in position

Inferior vena cava

Mike Courtney/Telectronics

The pacemaker, which contains the power source and circuitry to produce the electrical impulse, is implanted in the chest wall. The lead, which carries the impulse, *is threaded through the pulmonary vein and the electrode is wedged into the right ventricle (above). This marvel of miniaturization is not disfiguring (right).*

Putting in a pacemaker

Two sorts of pacing systems are used. The first is a temporary system. A pacing wire is passed through the skin via a special needle and into a large vein, usually around the shoulder. It is then passed into the right atrium, through the tricuspid valve and into the tip of the right ventricle, where it makes contact with the heart muscle. The position of the wire is followed on an X-ray so that it can be guided into the right place. If it is fixed to the skin, it is fairly unlikely to be dislodged. The other end of the wire is attached to a pacing box which remains outside the patient's body.

For a permanent system, the same principle is used. Once the wire is con-

nected to the pacing box, and the electrical connection between the wire and heart is shown to be adequate, the pacing box is sewn into a special pocket under the skin of the chest. Although the pacing box is only the size of a matchbox, it contains enough battery power to keep producing impulses for years – more than 10 years in some cases.

Pacing has probably saved many patients' lives. It has also prevented disabling symptoms such as recurrent blackouts. These problems tend to occur in the elderly, but age is no bar to having a pacemaker put in. The effect of pacing can be so beneficial to the well being of some elderly patients that a pacemaker will nearly always be tried. The object of a pacemaker in, say, patients in their nineties is not to postpone their death, but to relieve unpleasant symptoms.

Camera Press

The West German Chancellor, Helmut Schmidt, had a pacemaker fitted in 1981.

Paediatrics

Q I am due to give birth soon and feel slightly anxious about the first few weeks of caring for my new baby. Is there anyone I can talk to about this before leaving hospital?

A Yes. An ideal opportunity to discuss any worries, no matter how trivial they seem, is when the paediatrician examines your baby before you go home. He, or she, can answer any questions you may have, and thus help to reassure you before you leave.

Q I understand that newborn babies cannot see. When will my baby be able to see me?

A Babies can see as soon as they are born, and are instinctively interested in the human face. They focus best at about 30.5 cm (12 in), which is roughly the distance a breast-feeding baby is from his mother's face.

Q Our son was born five weeks early and had to be fed in an incubator for two weeks. Will he always be delicate?

A No. Premature babies usually need help with feeding at first, but once they have developed the ability to suck, they should grow as well as any other baby. There is no reason why your son should not be the same as every other child.

Q I got very angry with my three-month-old baby today when he would not stop crying, and shook him vigorously. I am afraid I might harm him. What should I do?

A Shaking babies hard can be very harmful, especially when they are so young. The blood vessels around the brain can be damaged causing a clot to form between the brain and skull. It is very important for you to find help so you can improve your relationship with your son. You can seek help through your local authority social services or general practitioner. Remember that your problem is not uncommon, and that there are a variety of experts available to give you assistance when you need it.

The branch of medicine concerned with the health and illnesses of children is called paediatrics. From the time a child is born the utmost is done to prevent, cure and alleviate disease.

A paediatrician is a doctor who cares for children from the moment they are born until they reach puberty. These age limits are not fixed and often a paediatrician has already been involved with the obstetrician before a baby is born if a problem is anticipated. Within the hospital the paediatrician works in conjunction with other specialists to care for children. They also work with other paediatricians at large centres specializing in rare problems.

The birth of a baby

Fortunately the vast majority of babies are entirely normal at birth and start to breathe spontaneously a few seconds after delivery. But in some cases, for instance with a forceps delivery or premature birth, a baby is more likely to have difficulty in breathing. Therefore a paediatrician is usually present at such times to give any necessary help.

As it is not always possible to predict which babies will have problems, a paediatrician is available at the hospital 24 hours a day. Even if a baby needs some encouragement to start breathing, once this is established almost all babies have no more trouble and are given back to their mothers before they are returned with them to the ward.

Special care baby units

About one in eight babies is admitted to a special care baby unit, usually for only a short time. The commonest reasons are that the baby is 'pre-term' (born more than three weeks before he or she was due), or that he has not grown as well as usual in the womb. Often these babies are too weak to suck properly and need to be fed through a tube for a few days. The

Thanks to the advances in medicine, most babies are not only born healthy but, with paediatric care, they also remain that way.

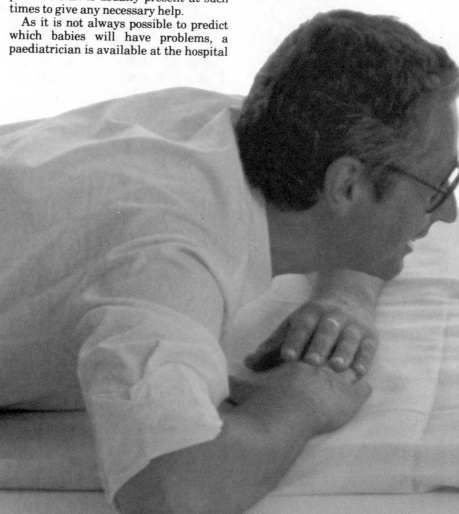

This child, who has a rare spinal problem, is being tested by a neuro-surgeon, who will work closely with a paediatrician.

Premature babies are often placed in incubators where their vital signs are monitored, and they are kept warm and fed.

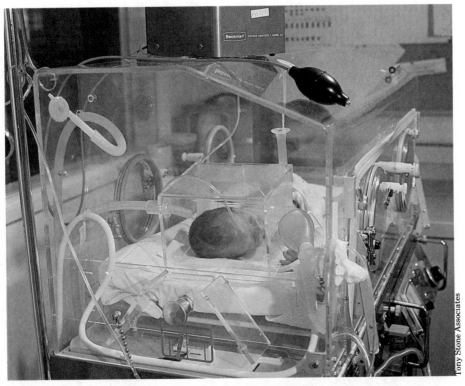

tube is threaded via the baby's nose or mouth into the stomach and milk passed through it. The babies are kept warm in the meantime in incubators.

Some babies born prematurely may weigh less than 1.4 kg (3 lb 5 oz). In order to help these babies survive and grow

normally a great deal of skill and complicated equipment is needed. Very tiny babies must have their breathing and heartbeat monitored continuously. They may also need to be given fluid into one of their veins instead of their stomachs, as well as having a ventilator.

It is important for the parents of a premature baby to get used to the special care unit and spend time with their baby. Even the smallest and illest babies can usually be fondled through an incubator porthole. As the babies grow stronger, parents can hold, help feed and care for them, in readiness for their homecoming.

Children in hospital

Most children who are admitted to hospital are brought by their parents as emergency cases. They may have had an accident at home or on the road, or need prompt treatment for respiratory disorders, appendicitis or bowel upsets. Other children go in for minor operations such as tonsillectomy or repair of a hernia. Otherwise they perhaps have problems such as difficulty with feeding or failure to grow properly which a period of observation and treatment in hospital can solve.

A stay in hospital is very likely to be a

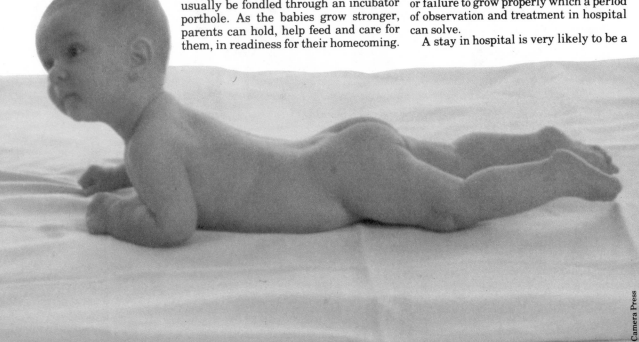

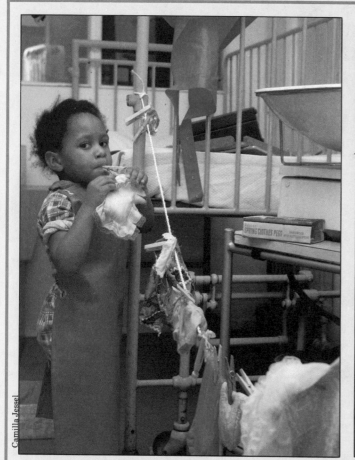

Camilla Jessel

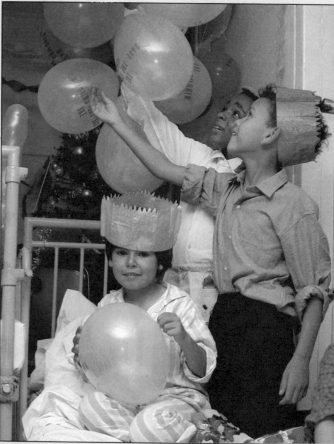

Camilla Jessel

Guidelines for children in hospital

Children are naturally anxious about their first encounter with a hospital, so it is best to prepare them beforehand so that they know what to expect. This way fears can be dealt with, and their stay can be made much more enjoyable.

● Explain to the child what a hospital is. If possible take him on a tour of the children's ward before he is admitted.

● Tell the child what is going to be done to him, and be honest if something will be painful. Don't be alarmist.

● When you are packing the child's bag let him choose some of his favourite things, such as a toy or comforter.

● Try to stay with the child in hospital if this is at all possible – otherwise visit frequently and bring along other members of the family. Children are welcome too.

● Be prepared for tears – they are a normal and healthy reaction. In most cases, the child will soon stop crying and begin to get interested in the activities in the ward. If problems persist, speak to the play therapist.

● Ask the staff on the ward any questions you have, however busy they seem. If you feel reassured you will give your child more confidence.

● Afterwards don't expect the child to be entirely fit – discharge only means he is well enough to be home.

● Expect a difficult period following his stay in hospital: dependence and bed-wetting are common but thankfully only temporary occurrences.

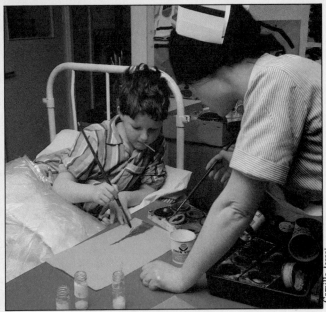

Camilla Jessel

Q I am worried about my daughter having her whooping cough immunization, as I heard that there can be side-effects. What do paediatricians now advise?

A An extensive survey has been done to correlate immunization with serious neurological (brain and nervous system) disease in children. This has shown that there are rarely serious complications with modern whooping cough injections. Immunization is recommended for all children unless there is a family history of neurological illness or seizures. If you are in doubt, check with your doctor.

Q My eight-month-old baby has a high temperature. I think it's because she's teething. How can I be sure?

A Almost every childhood complaint has been attributed to teething at some time. It may cause irritability and dribbling but never fever or convulsions. If your child has a fever it is important for your doctor to see her and find out the exact cause. Meanwhile keep her cool, give her liquid acetaminophen and plenty of fluids.

Q I am worried that my four-month-old son cannot hear properly. Is he too young to have his hearing tested?

A No, he isn't. If you are in any doubt, arrange to see the paediatrician or your family doctor at once. They will probably do some preliminary tests, and then arrange for your son to have a detailed examination by an audiometrist (hearing specialist).

Q I am concerned that my 18-month-old grand-daughter doesn't eat properly, but my daughter says there's nothing the matter. Who is right?

A Many children of this age lose interest in food as they test out their newly acquired skills, such as walking and talking. Their food requirement also lessens now as their growth rate slows down. As long as your grand-daughter has plenty of energy and is growing well, there is no need to worry.

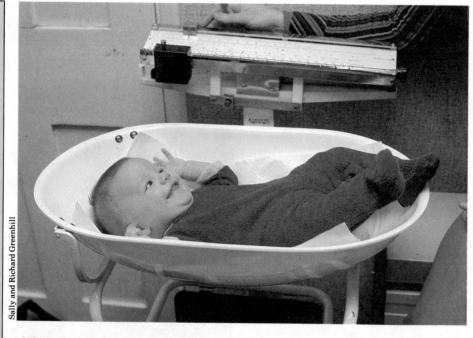

Sally and Richard Greenhill

child's first time away from home and parents. Over the last 30 years great efforts have been made to minimize the deep and lasting impression such an experience can make on a child.

Perhaps the most important change is that most children, irrespective of what is wrong with them, are admitted to wards where there are no adults and everything is geared to suit their particular needs.

Nowadays children's wards are bright and cheerfully decorated and filled with plenty of interesting things to do. It is routine for a play therapist to be present, as well as a teacher during term-time. Children are no longer expected to lie in bed all day, unless they are so ill that they prefer this. They are usually normally dressed and playing, and hard to distinguish from fit children visiting the ward.

Another important change has been in recognizing how vital it is for children, particularly the under-fives, to have their mothers or very familiar persons with them as much as possible. Mothers are encouraged to stay with their children in the hospital if this can be arranged. Also paediatric wards now have very relaxed attitudes towards visiting times and not only welcome parents but other children and members of the family.

Nevertheless a hospital stay can be a disturbing experience for a child, especially as some potentially painful or uncomfortable tests and medical procedures are inevitable. Often, fears and upsets are alleviated if children are allowed to talk about their worries. Young children may not be able to do this, but they can be encouraged to express themselves through stories and play.

Play therapists are expert at talking to

Tiny babies are weighed at frequent intervals to see if they are putting on weight and if a change of diet is needed.

children in this situation and helping them to voice their fears. It is important to identify the exact cause of their anxiety so that they can be reassured.

Child development

Children are continuously growing, physically, mentally and emotionally. It is an important part of paediatrics to observe these changes, identify problems if they occur and advise on how to deal with them.

The routine surveillance of most children is carried out by paediatricians and family doctors. The time of the examinations should be spaced so that children are seen at key points of their development—especially in the first two years of their life.

The first major check on babies is in the first week of life before leaving the hospital. This is primarily concerned with finding any congenital abnormalities, such as hip dislocation or heart disorders. There is a similar review at six weeks to ensure that the baby is growing well, and that there are still no congenital problems. Again, the hips and heart are looked at closely. This is a good opportunity for the mother to discuss with the paediatrician any problems of feeding, sleeping and coping with her new baby.

At about eight months the emphasis is on general development. By this time babies should be smiling, babbling and well aware of what is happening around them. Many are sitting and beginning to crawl. Hearing tests and a test for a

Preventive paediatrics

Age of child	6 weeks	2 months	4 months	6 months	15 months	18 months	2 years	4-5 years
Immunization		Triple vaccine (diphtheria, tetanus, whooping cough) Polio	Triple vaccine Polio	Triple vaccine Polio	Measles, mumps, rubella Tuberculin test	Triple vaccine Polio		Triple vaccine Polio
Surveillance checks	General examination for congenital defects growth, feeding, sleeping			Hearing, sight, overall development (at 6-12 months)		Overall development, especially walking, language, behaviour	Overall development, behaviour, vision, language	Pre-school assessment

squint should be done around this age.

The next examination is at about 18 months when most children are walking and starting to talk. At two, language skills, vision and behaviour are assessed, and readiness for school is assessed at about five years.

This scheme is designed to discover abnormalities as they arise, but no parent should feel obliged to wait for the next appointment if they are worried, particularly about vision and hearing.

Any problems the paediatrician finds are dealt with in collaboration with the family's general practitioner. These may be quite trivial and easy to treat such as diaper rash, a yeast infection or scabies. Other problems may be more complicated and need specialist help.

Of all the specialists and resources available the most appropriate ones must be chosen in each case. A child with a physical disorder, like a heart murmur, may be referred to a general paediatrician, while severe behaviour problems may require psychiatric help at a child guidance centre or hospital.

A child whose overall development gives cause for concern may be referred to a local assessment centre. Here a whole team of experts can meet and examine a child together. They may include paediatricians, specialists in hearing and vision, orthopaedic surgeons, physiotherapists, psychologists, teachers and speech therapists. They may be able to assess a child immediately or may need to admit him briefly to the children's ward for tests and closer observation. A plan for any further therapy can then be made.

Preventive medicine also includes immunizations of children and these are done as a matter of routine at the doctor's office. As well as major checkups, babies may attend frequently for weighing when they are small. These visits are usually arranged individually with the doctor.

A child's health and development are carefully monitored. This means a programme of immunization against disease at certain intervals (left), as well a regular physical examinations (below).

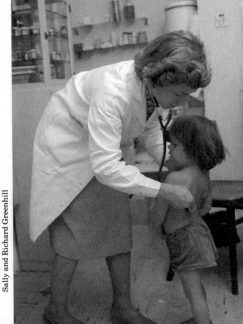

Paget's disease

Q I thought bones were dead like hair, so how can disease affect them?

A Bone cells are very much alive and they are continually breaking down existing bone and adding on new growth. In mature bones the rate of growth equals the rate of breakdown so there is no change in the overall size. Just like any other living cells in the body, they are susceptible to a variety of disease – Paget's disease is one of the most common.

Q My father had osteitis and said they knew because his head got bigger and bigger. Is that really one of the symptoms of the disease?

A Sometimes the skull is affected by this disease. The natural processes of growth and resorption of bone are speeded up and occasionally abnormal growth occurs faster than the breakdown. The skull then thickens and appears to grow larger.

People affected by the disease who regularly wear hats frequently complain of having to buy a larger size all the time.

Q Someone in my family suffers from osteitis. Does this mean that I am more likely to get the disease?

A It's still not certain whether the disease is genetic or not, but evidence has shown that it can run in families. In 1969 there was one family who actually experienced six separate cases of osteitis in three generations.

Q My neighbour keeps breaking his leg. It seems to happen for no reason at all – he doesn't fall or get knocked. Could he possibly have Paget's disease?

A There are several causes of bone weakness—all of which should be checked out by a doctor. Certainly, Paget's disease does cause the softening and weakening of bones which can bring about a spontaneous fracture without a person actually being involved in any violent type of accident.

Bones so fragile that they break on their own accord and an enlarged skull that pinches the brain – these are the worst symptoms of Paget's disease, a type of osteitis.

Osteitis exists in several forms, but by far the most common is Paget's disease, or osteitis deformans, where the bones are often deformed and weakened.

The disease was discovered by Sir James Paget in 1870. Much has been learned about the symptoms and treatment, but the causes of the disease still remain a mystery.

As many as three to four per cent of the population suffered from Paget's disease in the 19th century. Today the incidence has increased and in 1975 it was estimated that 13 per cent of the population over 40 years old suffered from the disease.

A strange fact that has been discovered is that the disease is more common in certain areas in England than anywhere else in the world.

Causes

Although research is continuing, it is not known what causes the sudden acceleration of bone growth and resorption in osteitis. As yet no genetic factor has been proved, but the disease does sometimes appear to run in families.

Symptoms

Many of the people suffering from Paget's disease have no symptoms at all. But sometimes they can be unbearably severe and complications can develop.

It is diagnosed on X-ray by the alternate light and dark areas of bone and the bones most commonly affected are the skull, the vertebrae of the backbone, the pelvis and the femur and tibia of the leg. Deformity in the long bones is most obvious – the bones bow outwards under the weight of the rest of the body as the bone loses its strength and softens. Strange irregularities in the bone structure show up on X-rays. A 'shepherd's crook' shaped lump is typical on

The irregular bone growth experienced in Paget's disease causes severe deformity of the affected limbs.

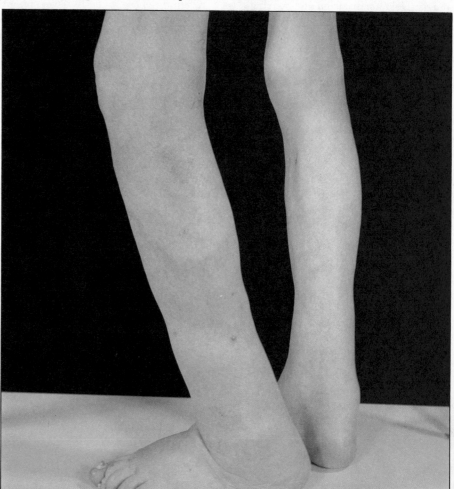

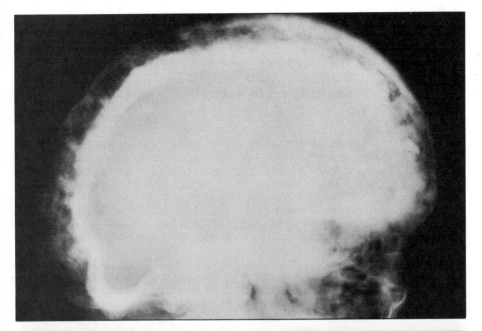

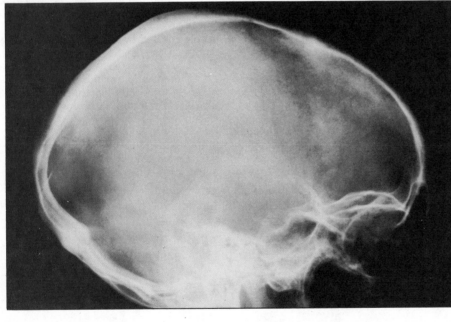

Goethe Institute

Thickening of the bones in the skull (above left) caused by Paget's disease, can be easily distinguished on X-ray from a normal skull (left). It is thought that Beethoven (above) went deaf as a result of this form of osteitis.

the top end of the femur. Also, the skull becomes lumpy in its appearance and also much thicker.

These changes occur because bone cells become super-active and bone resorption (the normal destructive process balanced by growth) proceeds at 10 to 20 times the normal rate. The new bone that is laid down is usually more fragile and less elastic. This means that a small knock can cause a fracture. In very bad cases bones become so weak that they break on their own.

Pain is one of the worst symptoms of osteitis; nerves squashed by the enlarging bone may be one cause, but changes in the actual bone structure cause stresses and strain that trigger the pain pathways of the body.

Dangers

Bone pressure on the nerves coming from the ears can cause deafness. Sometimes the same result occurs through deformation of the tiny sound transmitting bone structures in the ears. Beethoven's deafness was said to have been caused by Paget's disease.

Blindness can also be caused by bones pinching the optic nerves. But most of all, the bone at the base of the skull occasionally softens and sticks into an important part of the brain called the brain stem. The person may then lose control over vital functions such as breathing.

Treatment

In the past treatment has not been very satisfactory. Drugs are now available

that can control the symptoms of disease without the dangerous side-effects that accompanied early therapy.

A hormone called calcitonin is the most successful treatment to be given to people with Paget's disease. This is because the main problem in the disease is an imbalance in the function of bone growth and resorption (in normal bones this is a process which is going on all the time). Calcitonin helps by adjusting the balance between these two important processes to a normal level.

The effect of the drugs is that the rate of bone turnover drops and the temperature of the skin over the diseased bone falls back to normal. Often this drug will be effective against pain too. Injections have to be given daily and sometimes nausea is a side-effect.

Another drug called mithramycin can be used; just one dose gives one to two years free from disease. But liver damage can result.

Aspirin is still used but the high doses used can be poisonous.

Outlook

Paget's disease cannot be cured as such, but treatment aimed at giving sufferers a symptom-free life has reached a high standard. Also, there is great optimism about the outcome of future research into this distressing illness.

1475

Pain

Q Why is it that severe pain can make one pass out?

A The parts of the brain that receive and analyze painful stimuli from inside or outside the body have close connections with the parts which have overall control of blood circulation, the heartbeat and the condition of the peripheral blood vessels. Even small degrees of pain cause some change in pulse rate and/or blood pressure, but if the pain is severe the circulation may be swamped by these influences: the blood vessels dilate and the blood pressure drops enough to cause consciousness to be lost. This process is the same for any severe unpleasant stimulus, though people vary as to what degree of pain causes such a faint.

Q I have been told that acupuncture works only psychologically to relieve pain. Is this true?

A There is no doubt that psychological factors are very important in any method of pain relief, because of the considerable psychological component in our appreciation of pain. Moreover, it is likely that there is also a genuinely physiological mechanism at work in some methods of acupuncture.

Q Is it true that some people do genuinely feel pain more easily than others?

A Undoubtedly. The threshold above which a person interprets some stimulus as painful varies enormously both for psychological and physical reasons. For example, different people require different amounts of pain killers or local anaesthetics to relieve pains caused by identical stimuli.

Q Can chronic pain drive you mad?

A In the sense of becoming psychotic probably not, but severe depression can certainly result from prolonged pain. Often the personality seems to be changed as the pain takes over the unfortunate person's whole life. Fortunately such severe pain is not common.

Pain is familiar to most people in daily life. And it is important to recognize that it is the body's alarm system, alerting and teaching us to avoid harm and to seek attention for painful illnesses.

Minor degrees of pain are part of the repertoire of our sensory contact with the outside world and with the workings of our bodies. Through the experience of pain we learn to avoid unpleasant elements in our world – though hopefully it is the prospect of pain that warns us after we have had some experience of it. In disease, more severe and distressing pain arises from the persistent presence of some harmful stimulus in part of our bodies or, on occasion, the malfunction, due to some kind of damage, of the nerve fibres which carry and analyze painful stimuli within the nervous system.

A large section of the nervous system participates in the sensation which we call pain – from the peripheral nerves to the most sophisticated thinking areas of the cerebral cortex. There are many different types of pain: these depend on the variety of stimuli by which they are caused, and the way in which these stimuli are analyzed by the nervous networks in the spinal cord and brain. In addition, cultural and social factors play an enormous role in determining our mind's response to the perception of pain.

The purpose of pain

The ability to feel pain is vital to our well-being. This can be seen from situations in which the whole or parts of the body lose their ability to discern this sensation. In leprosy, for example, the nerves to the hands and feet are damaged so that pain is no longer felt there; as a result, sufferers damage their hands and feet continually without feeling pain.

Similarly, a very few people are born unable to feel pain at all and they must be carefully protected from injuring themselves – injuries that would damage anyone who did not heed the warning messages conveyed by the pain system. We do not go around touching boiling hot saucepans because the few times we have done this the pain has firmly reminded us of the tissue damage that can occur.

Pain from our internal organs warns us in the same way of the presence of disease. Indigestion following overeating warns us to be less greedy with the next meal.

Unfortunately, the paradox of the situation is that while the most distressing aspect of disease may be the pain, it

Pain can be especially distressing to a child – even a trivial injury can trigger tears. A kiss and cuddle can be highly effective 'treatment'.

Ron Sutherland

The pathways of pain

Thalamus

Cerebral cortex

Fast conducting pathway of pain to the brain

Midbrain

Slower, analytical pathway of pain to the brain

Medulla where detailed analysis of pain begins

Cervical spinal cord

Message sent to remove hand from painful stimulus

Elaine Keenan

Ron Sutherland

is that pain, its character and position, which enables doctors to detect the root cause of the complaint and effect treatment. For example, when a person has abdominal pain it is very dangerous to damp it down immediately with pain-killers, since this may mask the further development of painful symptoms which herald the presence of some serious disorder. Naturally, once the doctor is sure of a diagnosis the symptom can be treated as vigorously as possible.

How pain comes about

Painful stimuli inside and outside our bodies excite otherwise unspecialized nerve endings in the skin and elsewhere. These nerve endings are attached to

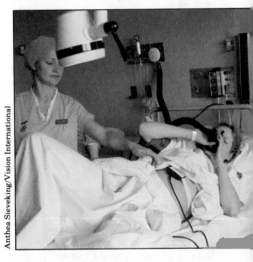

Anthea Sieveking/Vision International

When labour pains are at their worst they can be eased by inhaling a mixture of nitrous oxide and oxygen. The diagram shows the pathways of pain. The picture (below left) depicts dull pain – a persistent earache; (below right) a sharp pain is caused by contact with a hot iron.

nerves of two different types. One is fast-conducting and conveys its information rapidly to the spinal cord; the other also takes its information to the spinal cord but in a more leisurely fashion. This helps to distinguish between two types of pain – the immediately felt – and therefore reacted to – tapping or pricking pain and the deep, dull, aching pain.

These nerve endings make many contacts with the network of fibres in the spinal cord which are responsible for the initial analysis of our sensations and pain in particular. A second nerve fibre then takes this more organized information upwards to the brain. Again this happens by two different pathways: one makes fairly directly for the thalamus (the main sensory relay station deep in the brain) while the other leads a more meandering course, making many connections with

Q Can a husband really feel the pain of his wife's childbirth?

A Probably not. But if a husband is very close to his wife his brain may synthesize some of the distress (if any) of childbirth but this is unusual. More particularly, not feeling anything like this does not mean that the husband does not care.

Q Surely when someone loses pain sensation in a leg due to a disorder of the nerve this is a good thing?

A No. In such a situation the warning value of pain is lost and that person will not notice minor injuries, which may then progress to ulcers which can cause serious damage to the limb. Pain is a helpful sign, giving warning of actual or potential damage to tissues.

Q Is there any truth in the theory that twins, although separated by many miles can feel the pain of each other's injuries?

A No, there is no real evidence that this happens and no theoretical way in which it could.

Q I have seen programmes on TV showing some religious initiates walking over beds of red hot coals, with no shoes on. Do such people feel no pain?

A At the time, probably no. The situation is similar to the soldier who may feel no pain from even quite severe injuries sustained in the heat of battle. If the mind is sufficiently diverted either by the induction of a religious trance or by the fear and excitement of a battle, the brain does not pay sufficient attention for the painful sensations to reach consciousness even though messages may be reaching the spinal cord about the unpleasant events happening. The other point is that there is considerable cultural pressure on such religious initiates not to show to the world their pain, even should it penetrate the barrier their minds erect against feeling it.

The cultural pressure on people to resist showing pain is probably simply an example of the control societies demand of our emotional expression in general.

centres in the brainstem before also arriving at the thalamus. This enables the cortex (the part of the brain with which we actually perceive the pain) to obtain both direct, fast reports of the painful situation plus more slowly arriving but more heavily analyzed information by the slow pathway.

The thalamus, which analyzes this information for presentation to the cerebral cortex, has rich connections with the areas of the brain concerned with the maintenance of emotional tone and those concerned with arousal. So before our perceiving brain receives any information – but especially painful stimuli – it is heavily tinged by our emotional state and affected by our level of arousal.

The final arbiter as to whether we perceive pain is the cerebral cortex. It seems that large areas of this part of the brain participate in this complex perception. The frontal lobes, especially those parts of them concerned with the analysis of emotions (that is, the parts of the frontal lobes which connect with the 'limbic system'), seem to be important for our perception of painful stimuli as unpleasant. People who have lost this part of their brains report that they can feel pain but are not upset by it. The parietal lobes of the brain seem to be important in the localization of the painful stimulus but they also participate in perception of the sensations associated with pain.

Different types of pain

Skin pain: this is usually well localized and is either of a pricking or burning quality, or subtle combinations of the

Some cultures make a virtue of pain: in this Thai Pusau ceremony a celebrant has both cheeks pierced by a metal rod.

two, according to whether the fast or slowly conducting nerve fibres are stimulated or both.

Internal pain: this is more variable but tends to be much more poorly localized though perceived as deeper and often of a duller quality. The stimulation of combinations of different sensory fibres may produce a variety of stabbing, pressing or constricting pains which can be felt emanating from our internal organs.

Referred pain: pain coming from any internal organs may seem to be coming from areas of the body some distance from the actual position of that organ. This is because the nerves from these organs are received by, and their messages analyzed by, parts of the spinal cord which also deal with those areas to which the pain seems to be referred. Thus pain coming from the heart is felt in the centre of the chest but also in the left arm and in the jaw, the pain messages spilling over in their spinal analyzing centres into neighbouring zones.

These facts are of great use to doctors who, by careful questioning of a person with a pain, can usually get a clear idea of the organ involved. Not all organs refer their pains to distant sites, but many do so in characteristic distributions.

Pain from the nervous system: damage to the peripheral nerves themselves may be the cause of pain instead of the stimulation of these nerves by harmful stimuli, either chemical or physical. Thus pressure on the nerve (the median nerve) in the wrist may commonly cause pain and tingling in the hand which, again because of the connections in the spinal cord, may spread up the arm to other parts of the body.

Slipped discs in the spine can cause direct pressure on the sensory nerves as they enter the spinal cord and here, since the nerve being pressed upon carries impulses from the back of the leg, the pain is felt by the sufferer as going down the back of the leg.

Damage to the spinal cord itself, from pressure due to tumours or inflammations such as multiple sclerosis, also causes pain which may be referred to the part of the body whose sensations are analyzed by that segment of the cord which has been affected.

Damage to other parts of the central nervous system may also cause pain. In particular, damage to the thalamus due to minor strokes may cause very unpleasant sensations and pain since the nerves organizing the incoming stimuli are disorganized and interpret ordinary sensations as painful.

Phantom pains: when an arm or a leg has been amputated, for whatever reason, the nerves remain in the stump. If they are stimulated by swelling or scar-

Wounded soldiers may experience a delayed reaction to pain: only when they are in a safe place will its full intensity be felt.

ring of the stump, the brain will register the pain as if it was coming from the lost leg or arm. After a while the brain usually reorganizes its perceptions so that the pain, if present, is actually felt in the stump: but initially the site of the pain is perceived according to where the nerves usually come from.

Psychological aspects of pain

As large areas of the nervous system participate in our feelings and responses to painful stimuli, it is not surprising that the state of a person's mind is an important factor in his or her perception of pain. This state of mind is strongly influenced by the situation in which the pain occurs and the cultural and social background against which our attitudes to pain have grown up.

In the heat of a battle, a soldier may feel no pain even though he has suffered substantial injuries because his mind may be so occupied with the battle. Later when the wound is being dressed the pain may be severe, although the injury is unchanged. With practitioners of yoga in India, the mind may be so diverted away from the painful stimuli by contemplation of other things that what appear to be great feats of endurance – such as lying on beds of nails – can be achieved.

The threat of injury – and the pain associated with it – is a fact of life in a contact sport like soccer.

It is likely that such people are not actually feeling the pain in the same way as we would, rather than enduring it: they have managed to divert their minds from the unpleasant significance of the stimuli which are undoubtedly reaching their brains.

The other side of this coin is the psychological effect that pain can have on us. Prolonged severe pain can start a vicious cycle whereby the mental ability to cope with pain is progressively eroded and often appears to change a person's personality. It makes them pay attention to the pain to a greater degree, perceiving it as more and more severe.

It is therefore wrong to consider pain as only being 'in the mind' because all pain is a mental process to a greater or lesser extent, depending on the circumstances.

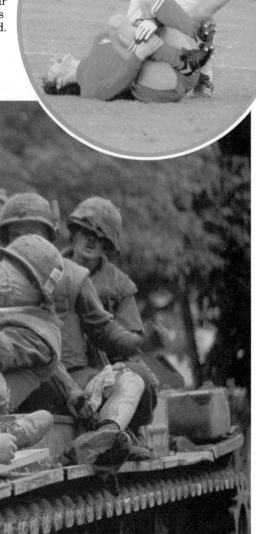

John Olson/Colorific!

Mick Alexander

Painkillers

Q Is it true that taking low doses of aspirin is good for the heart and circulation?

A Yes, there is an increasing amount of evidence to suggest that aspirin may help to prevent heart attacks if taken in very low doses. However, the value of aspirin is not definitely established and since it can cause stomach trouble it should not be taken for this purpose at the moment. Doctors are hoping to solve this question as a result of the large studies which are being carried out. Half the doctors over 55 in England took it as part of a trial!

Q Does acupuncture really work as a painkiller?

A It certainly does work, although we are not yet sure why. In China, dentists will drill and fill teeth on people anaesthetized by acupuncture—a good test of its effectiveness. It is possible that the physical effects are aided by a 'placebo' effect, that is, the patient believes the treatment will work and so it does.

Q I'm pregnant – should I use painkillers for backache or headache?

A Because pregnant women ingest so many drugs during their pregnancy in the normal course of things – caffeine in tea and coffee, nicotine in cigarette smoke, alcohol – it is often very difficult to point a finger at a particular drug and blame it for a particular abnormality, especially when a problem can arise from a combination rather than an individual drug. While new drugs are now tested very carefully for effects on the foetus, we do not know for sure the effects of many over-the-counter painkillers. Any substance taken by a pregnant woman will pass to the foetus, especially during the first three months. After that, some drugs will be screened out by the placenta, but not all. As a general rule, then, drugs – even mild painkillers – should be avoided during the first three months of pregnancy. After that, try to take only medicines prescribed by your doctor.

Most of us take pain-killing drugs at some time or other. How do they work and should we use them every time the stress of modern living causes discomfort?

The medical term for a pain-relieving drug is an analgesic. Doctors usually divide pain-killing drugs into two categories – narcotic and non-narcotic. Narcotics, such as morphine and heroin, which are derived from opium, and their synthetic relations like pethedine and methadone, act principally on the brain and often produce drug dependence. Non-narcotic drugs, such as aspirin, are rarely addictive as such and act on the site of the pain. Narcotic drugs are usually used in highly controlled conditions such as in hospital, to give relief for pain in internal organs. The non-narcotic drugs are used to control pain felt in the joints, muscles, bones or skin.

Pain relieving drugs were once obtained from natural sources—morphine, for example, from the opium poppy. Purified opium preparations are still used, but drugs are now usually prepared synthetically.

The best known painkillers are aspirin, acetaminophen, codeine and morphine. Non-narcotic drugs such as the first two are available over the counter and are commonly used to relieve headaches or pains like premenstrual stomach cramps. The painkillers we buy from drugstores are all combinations of aspirin, acetaminophen and codeine, sometimes with the addition of a stimulant such as caffeine. But they have different effects on our bodies and are far from simple in their operation.

Aspirin
Aspirin is probably the best known and most widely used drug (see pp 98-99). Not only does it relieve pain, it also reduces fever and has an anti-inflammatory effect on joints. This is why doctors often prescribe aspirin for influenza – not necessarily to kill any pain the patient may be feeling – which is often more discomfort than pain—but to reduce the temperature and to help ease the aches in joints often experienced in such an illness. Aspirin is used for rheumatism, often over extended periods, for this anti-inflammatory property.

However, aspirin can be extremely dangerous to some people in certain circumstances. It is an irritant and can cause stomach pain, with nausea and vomiting. But far more important, if swallowed whole, an aspirin tablet will not just irritate the stomach lining but may even cause bleeding. For this reason, aspirin should never be taken on an empty stomach without a drink of water. Aspirin can be extremely dangerous to old people on poor diets, especially if they are low in iron, and to patients who are weak from an illness. You can even develop superficial ulcers in the stomach from aspirin use without realizing it, and this in turn can lead to blood loss and anaemia.

If you do take aspirin, always take the soluble form, dissolved in warm water and with plenty of liquids, and preferably not on an empty stomach. Aspirin in soluble form is not only more easily absorbed through the stomach lining into the bloodstream without causing irritation; it also is absorbed far more rapidly so producing the desired effects far more quickly. Some of the commercial preparations contain sodium bicarbonate and 'fizz' when dissolved in water. This is not just a commercial gimmick: sodium bicarbonate is an alkali and so helps to prevent irritation.

Some people may react badly to aspirin, and others may have a definite allergy. Since aspirin is present in many commercial drugs, either as aspirin or under chemical compound terms such as acetylsanide, it is important to read the list of ingredients on preparations you buy for mild illnesses, to check that you are not giving it by mistake to someone who is allergic to it, or to someone who suffers from indigestion.

Other common analgesics
If, for any reason, a patient should not take aspirin, acetaminophen is often a good alternative. Acetaminophen is also a mild pain reliever and can reduce the temperature, although it has no effect on inflammation and this is of little use in rheumatism. It does not irritate the stomach lining and thus may be used for abdominal pain. However, acetaminophen can affect the function of the kidneys and the liver and should not be taken in high doses over long periods.

Codeine is an opium-derived drug, often used as part of anti-diarrhoea and cough suppressant medicines. As well as being a mild pain reliever, it slows down the action of the bowel and supresses the cough centre in the brain. Codeine is rarely used on its own but is often combined with other drugs, commonly

Common painkillers

	Uses	Dangers	Long term use	Contra indications
Aspirin	Mild painkiller; brings down temperature and reduces inflammation. Good for headaches, discomfort from colds and influenza or simple pains like backache.	Irritates stomach lining; can causes ulcers and bleeding.	Non addictive, but do not take regularly without doctor's advice.	Should not be taken by people with stomach problems. Do not take on an empty stomach or without water.
Acetaminophen	Mild painkiller. Used similarly to aspirin; can also be used for stomach aches.	Can cause kidney or liver damage if taken in high doses for a long time.	Use of large doses can cause kidney damage.	Should not be given to patients suffering from kidney or liver problems.
Distalgesic	Painkiller available on prescription; contains acetaminophen and morphine-derived dextropropoxyphene. Stronger than the above.	Can cause kidney damage.	Can be addictive and cause kidney damage.	Should not be given to patients suffering from liver or kidney problems.
Codeine	Painkiller available on prescription; often combined with aspirin and acetaminophen. Similar to the above.	As with aspirin and acetaminophen, and may also cause lightheadedness.	Heavy and long-term use can be addictive and cause kidney damage. Slightly constipating.	As aspirin and acetaminophen.

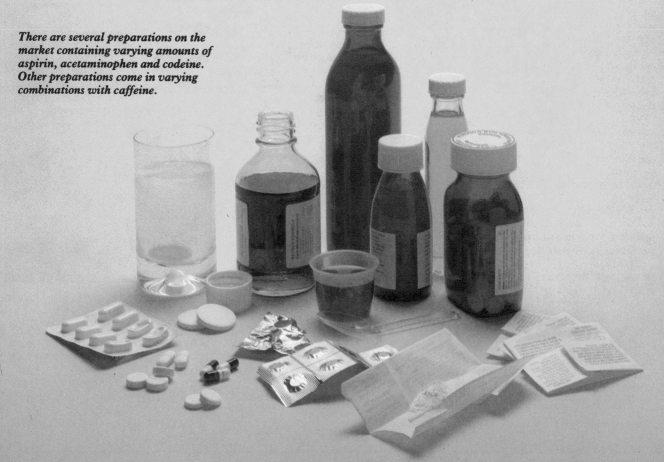

There are several preparations on the market containing varying amounts of aspirin, acetaminophen and codeine. Other preparations come in varying combinations with caffeine.

Phil Babb

Q I occasionally get blinding headaches that make me feel ill. A couple of aspirin have no effect. Should I take a larger dose?

A A blinding 'headache' with nausea is quite a good description of migraine. It is often difficult to tell the difference but the classic symptoms of migraine are a headache on one side of the head accompanied by nausea and vomiting. There are often visual disturbances (flashing lights of 'rippling' effects) and slurred speech.

Migraine may respond to aspirin or acetaminophen, but often these drugs fail. There are other preparations which, if taken as soon as possible after the migraine starts can help, but they should not be taken without first seeing a doctor.

Q In the case of an overdose, is it enough to make the person vomit, to get rid of the painkilling drugs?

A While immediate action is often, obviously, necessary in the case of overdose, never try to look after the patient on your own – always call an ambulance. You may be able to void the drugs before they are absorbed, but after some painkillers have entered the bloodstream (and depending on the state of the person and how they were taken, this can be very quickly indeed) the damage can be widespread and only amenable to medical help. Acetaminophen, for instance, can cause liver damage that kills several days after the overdose. The sufferer can show very few signs of damage for many hours before lapsing into coma.

Q My husband refuses to take drugs for a headache – he insists alcohol is a much better painkiller. Is he right?

A Alcohol does work as a painkiller to some extent. It relaxes and sedates many parts of the brain, and so can mask the signals of pain being sent from one site of an injury. A headache caused by tension can be relieved both physically and emotionally by a drink, as the alcohol relaxes the drinker. But in cases of injury or shock, alcohol can be positively dangerous and should never be used as a painkiller.

Phil Babb

aspirin and acetaminophen. It increases their effects, and adds a mild pain-relieving action on the brain while aspirin or acetaminophen on the other hand affects the site of the pain itself.

Morphine is made from opium. If taken

Raspberry tea is sometimes claimed to be beneficial for relieving pain associated with childbirth or menstruation.

repeatedly it becomes addictive, and the pain-killing effect lessens as the patient builds up a tolerance to the drug. Despite this problem morphine is the most effective pain-killer available to the doctor, and is used to treat almost every sort of disease.

Pain should be looked on rather like a burglar alarm. It would be foolish and harmful to switch off the alarm and then leave the burglars rampaging through your house: so in most cases the cause rather than the symptom should be sought and cured. But, just as many burglar alarms go off because of passing interference we sometimes feel pain for temporary and passing reasons which do not need the care of a doctor. In these cases, the right painkiller is necessary and beneficial. However, it is not advisable to continue taking over-the-counter painkillers for longer than two to three days. If the pain persists, medical advice should be sought.

TAKE CARE

Points to watch with painkillers

Ron Sutherland

● All analgesics cause a certain amount of drowsiness—you must be careful if you are driving or handling machinery while taking them.
● Analgesics can be harmful if taken over a long period of time. If you are in constant pain consult a doctor.
● All tablets, including analgesics, should be kept in childproof containers and locked in a medicine chest; children are notoriously curious about pills.

● Be careful about taking painkillers if you are already on other drugs.
● Do not take painkillers with alcohol.
● Always take painkillers with water and, if possible, not on an empty stomach.
● Check with a pharmacist or doctor if you are in doubt about the correct dose for children. Soluble painkillers, dissolved in water, are the most suitable and easily administered for them.